THE

Uncovering Divine Providence

HIDDEN

in major events of the 20th century

HAND

YAAKOV
ASTOR ✦

THE HIDDEN HAND
Uncovering Divine Providence
in major events of the 20th century

© 2007 Yaakov Astor

ISBN: 978-1-932443-79-0

Editor: Toby Cohen
Proofreader: Hadassa Goldsmith
Design and layout: Justine Elliott

THE JUDAICA PRESS, INC.
123 Ditmas Avenue / Brooklyn, NY 11218
718-972-6200 / 800-972-6201
info@judaicapress.com
www.judaicapress.com

Manufactured in the United States of America

Dedicated to the loving memory
of my father,

Chaim Benyamin ben Yaakov Reuven, a"h,

who imbued me with a love of history
and an intuition for *hashgachah*

Rabbi S.F. Zimmerman
3 Cedar Lane
Monsey, N.Y. 10952

שרגא פייבל הלוי זיממערמאן
קהל בני אשכנז
מאנסי נוא יארק

וויף ה' פ' דברים תשס"א

לכ' ידידי היקר חכם וסופר ר' יעקב אסטרייך ני'

The Torah teaches us (*Devarim* 32:7)

זכר ימות עולם בינו שנות דר-דר

It is incumbent upon us to remember the history of the world and attempt to understand the lessons of all the generations. Your enlightening book, *The Hidden Hand*, is a valuable aid to us in this important endeavor. It relates the details of well-known historical events in the last century and analyzes them with uncanny insight and wisdom, illustrating the Divine Providence that guided them. It serves both as an interesting book to read for pleasure and as a textbook to be studied in depth. I strongly encourage everyone alike to purchase *The Hidden Hand* and utilize it both ways.

Rashi (ibid) says if we remember the good Hashem bestowed upon us in the past, we will understand the future salvations that Hashem can grant us. May we merit seeing this in our day and generation.

הנני הח"ק וקמ"ה לכ' וסיום
סרגא פייבל הלוי זיממערמאן אב"ד

[stamp:] שרגא פייבל הלוי זיממערמאן
רב ואב"ד
קהל בני אשכנז
מאנסי, נ.י.

Tel: (845) 356-7939 ~ Fax: (845) 425-5881

YatedNe'eman

53 OLYMPIA LANE • MONSEY, NY 10952 • PHONE: 845.369.1600 • FAX: 845.369.6397

The *Medrash* in *Parshas Vayeishev* [*parsha* 85] states that at the time the brothers sold Yosef, the *shevotim* were occupied with the sale of Yosef, Yosef was overcome with *sak* and *taanis* - grief at his predicament; Reuvein was occupied with his *sak* and *taanis* – repenting; while Yaakov was occupied with his *sak* and *taanis* - mourning the loss of his beloved son. *Hakadosh Boruch Hu*, however, was occupied with creating the light of *Moshiach*, and thus the *posuk* says, "*Vayehi ba'eis hahi vayeired Yehudah…*"

We don't have the benefit of seeing the entire picture. To any outside observer, it appears as if the world is full of tragedy and hovering at the precipice of destruction. The brothers have sold Yosef into an uncertain future. Reuvein mourns, Yosef mourns and Yaakov mourns, but G-d has other plans. A time that to all outward appearances is bleak beyond belief is really a time in which G-d is preparing the light of *Moshiach*.

Often times, we look around us and see desolation and destruction. We see ill winds blowing from Iran, Iraq, Gaza, Yerushalayim, and other portents of danger, yet we must dig deeper. We must have a deeper vision and recognize that if we scratch beneath the surface, we will merit the revelation of the light of *Moshiach* for which *Hakadosh Boruch Hu* is preparing the world.

Moshe Rabbeinu asked Hashem (*Shemos* 33:13), "*Hodieni nah es derachecha*, show me your ways." Hashem responded to him that, "*Veraisah es achorai ufanei ahl yeira'u*, you can see my back but not my front…" An explanation is offered that man cannot understand what G-d will do before it is done; we have no comprehension of what is really transpiring as history unfolds. It is only with the benefit of hindsight that we can begin to understand and appreciate G-d's handiwork

Yaakov Astor's book, *The Hidden Hand*, examines history and traces the hand of G-d in some of the past century's seminal events. Based on his very popular and well-received articles, it contains remarkable lessons to Jews of all ages, teaching us, perhaps above all, not to take history at face value. As he traces events we all thought we knew and understood, the Divine bearing on the course of human events becomes readily apparent. These lessons are eternal, transcend time and are an inspiration to all.

Pinchos Lipschutz

"The heart of a king is like streams of water in the
hand of Hashem (G-d). He directs it wherever He wishes."

(MISHLEI 21:1)

"By examining his past history, every person
can discover a great network of intricate plan and
purpose, which makes him aware of Hashem's
constant guidance of the individual's footsteps.
By examining the events of Mankind's history, one becomes
aware of Hashem's guidance of the affairs of nations."

(RABBI AVIGDOR MILLER)

"One night in 1952 during the Presidential campaign,
Dwight Eisenhower confided something
to one of his advisers, a close friend, Senator Frank Carlson.
And Eisenhower told him that during the war
when he was commanding the Allied forces in Europe,
he'd had a startling and vivid spiritual experience—
he had actually felt the hand of G-d guiding him,
felt the presence of G-d ..."

(PRESIDENT RONALD REAGAN, REMARKS AT THE ANNUAL
NATIONAL PRAYER BREAKFAST, FEBRUARY 6, 1986)

"Certainly it was unexpected [my success as a leader],
but again I felt—forgive me for saying so—
that I was serving as the instrument, albeit unworthy,
of the plan of Providence."

(WINSTON CHURCHILL)

"... Providence facilitated [our] success,
and Providence doomed [us]."

(ALBERT SPEER, HITLER'S ARMAMENTS MINISTER)

Contents

PREFACE

This is not a Jewish history book. It is a book that presents general history—specifically, significant events of the twentieth century—from a Torah-based, Jewish perspective. Along the way, history specific to Jews is mentioned, but the main thrust is general history with a twist—viewed through the magnifying lens of a Torah perspective.

Studying general history, Rabbi Avigdor Miller tells us, has Torah value:

> By examining his past history, every person can discover
> a great network of intricate plan and purpose, which makes
> him aware of *Hashem's* constant guidance of the individual's
> footsteps. By examining the events of Mankind's history, one
> becomes aware of *Hashem's* guidance of the affairs of nations.
> (*Rejoice O Youth*, p. 347)

These words imply that we should study our individual past, as well as all Jewish history, and the history of other "nations," too. Today we need even greater vigilance in such study, because we live in a society where the long arm of the media reaches into even the most insular homes. Authors, journalists and historians who are often blind to, or antagonistic toward, the Torah ideology of a G-d who is intimately involved in human affairs dominate the presses and airwaves. Even the most benign general history books (such as those typically used in our children's schools) typically lack a Torah perspective. All this has a subtle (and sometimes not-so-subtle) effect on our lives and the lives of our children. Therefore, I have endeavored to write a book that takes well-known events of the past century and reframes them through a Torah perspective, using principles imparted by our Sages about the inner dynamics of history.

Of course, it is presumptuous to claim to know the dynamics of *Hashem's* guidance in human affairs, as it says:

"As the heavens are higher than the earth, so are My ways higher than your ways and My thoughts than your thoughts." (*Yeshayahu* 55:9)

Nevertheless, according to Rabbi Miller, it is possible to discern what an event may mean in a general way:

Hashem's plan is too grand for us to comprehend. When Moses requested, "Let me know Your ways" (*Shemos* 33:13), he was granted this privilege, according to one opinion of our Sages; but others of the Sages state that even Moses was not successful in attaining this knowledge (*Berachos* 7a). But in a general way, by following the principles expounded by the Sages, we are able to discern the general plan. (*Rejoice O Youth*, p. 266)

Hashem wants us to learn from the events He orchestrates. He doesn't want us to think they happen randomly.[1] And although we may be unable to recognize what is happening "behind the scenes," the Torah tells us things are happening.

The purpose of this book is to give readers a new (or sharper) lens with which to view events in a more Torah-like way; a lens that stimulates, enables and enhances their ability to read both past history and today's news, with an eye toward possible *hashgachah*, the "hidden hand" in world events.

• Letters from G-d

The Torah word for "Divine Providence" is *hashgachah*,[2] which literally translates, "to see over" or "oversee." It means that *Hashem* "watches over" events, i.e., they don't happen independently of Him, without His knowledge or ability to intervene. This, in fact, is the first of Maimonides' Thirteen Principles of Faith:

... *Hashem* alone is the cause behind everything that has occurred, does occur and will occur.

Rav Shimon Schwab summarized it this way:

> The doctrine of *hashgachah pratis* lies at the heart of our
> entire *emunah* (faith). It teaches that man's life on earth is
> not subject to coincidence and happenstance; rather, all of
> man's activities, his weal and his woe, are closely supervised
> by *Hashem* .... (*Rav Schwab on Iyov*, pp. 20-21, 27)

Coincidence has been described as "a letter sent by G-d ...
anonymously." The Torah viewpoint is that no matter how unjust
and haphazard things seem on the surface, there are no random or
chance occur-rences. There is no such thing as "coincidence."

Everything happens with *hashgachah*, closely supervised by
Hashem. Some *hashgachah* is more obvious than others. Some may
be practically impenetrable. Nevertheless, everything happens with
hashgachah.

The events in this book are meant to read like "anonymous
letters from *Hashem*." Even if the wording of the "letter" is virtually
indecipherable, as if it were in some obscure "code"—so to speak—
nevertheless, its existence is hard to deny. Some events will seem
quite compelling. Some obviously contain an extraordinary series
of "coincidences" and/or oddities that clearly point to *hashgachah*.
D-Day, for example, required such a remarkable linking of events
that the man most qualified to comment on it, General Dwight D.
Eisenhower, said he "felt the hand of G-d guiding him."[3]

Other events may not look as compelling at first glance, but, for
example, may have occurred on a particular date that, to the Jewish
world, is loaded with meaning and implications. Whether the
hashgachah is more compelling or less so, at the very least I have
endeavored to find Torah lessons that can be derived from the event.

WARNING: THE DANGER OF THIS STUDY

It must be noted that there are inherent dangers in attempting to
study events with an eye for *hashgachah*. First, in the absence of a

true prophet, all such attempts must be classified as speculation. There are degrees of speculation: at the high end, it is informed, with a basis in reason and/or Torah. But in the final analysis, speculation is just that—speculation.

The first danger, therefore, is assuming that one's speculation of an event is correct. However, I do not believe that this means we should avoid looking for *hashgachah*; rather, when we do, we should do so with all due diligence and genuine humility.

Second, it is easy to make the mistake of assuming that since everything happens with *hashgachah* and *Hashem* retains ultimate control, having faith means that events will always turn out the way we want (or think we want). The Chazon Ish refutes this way of thinking in his classic treatise on the meaning of faith in the Torah perspective:

> An age-old mistake resides in the hearts of many with regard to *bitachon* (faith or trust[4]) … that when a person is confronted by any situation and his future is uncertain—with two possible paths [one good and the other not] before him—then he is required to rest assured that it will be good. [They claim that] if he will be doubtful and plan for the opposite, then he is lacking in *bitachon*.

> This is incorrect, for unless the future has been clarified by prophecy, the future is not definite, for who can know *Hashem's* judgment or His deeds? Rather, *bitachon* involves the belief that there is no coincidence in the world and that every occurrence under the sun is by *Hashem's* proclamation. (*Emunah Uvitachon*)[5]

The Torah belief in an All-Powerful G-d does *not* imply that things will necessarily turn out the way we think we want them to turn out. Rather, it is the belief that "there is no coincidence in the world" and that "every occurrence under the sun is by *Hashem's* proclamation." This means that sometimes things can turn out seemingly unfavorably. People die, evil takes over (at least temporarily; long enough to cause enormous harm), a Holocaust takes place. In an authentic Torah view, such events are no less "*Hashem's* proclamation" than the birth of a baby, the downfall of evil or the survival of the Jewish people and rejuvenation of Torah in the post-Holocaust world.

Several chapters touch on the theological puzzle regarding the existence of evil in a universe where a benevolent G-d retains absolute control over human destiny.[6] To address this topic more fully, a follow-up book is in progress, with a specific focus on the Holocaust. In this book the majority of events have an ostensibly good outcome. However, this should not be construed to mean that manifest good always triumphs over manifest evil.

For example, the extraordinary string of events that turned D-Day into an Allied victory cannot necessarily be said to prove that *Hashem* manipulated events to bring about the downfall of Nazi Germany. One can make a counter-argument that if *Hashem* were truly in control, how could He allow the Nazis to rise to power in the first place? And if extraordinary events helped D-Day become an Allied victory, why weren't there extraordinary events to prevent the Nazi conquest of Europe in 1940?[7]

The point is *not* that events will necessarily conspire to bring about the outcome we hope for and believe is good. *Hashem* always retains the ability to do so, of course, but for reasons known ultimately only to Him, He may not do so. The point is that even in the modern world, where sophisticated technology and scientific knowledge have enabled unprecedented human control over Nature, there is invariably an unpredictable element, which ultimately makes the outcome more than just a product of human will. This element, of course, is the Divine Will and manifests itself as *hashgachah*. Rabbi Elie Munk summarizes this thought eloquently:

> Where man sees only the effect of blind chance, Judaism recognizes the action of providential intervention. It manifests itself as an immaterial factor, independent of

human will, coming from a supernatural sphere. It is interwoven in the fabric of our economic, social, scientific, or cultural activities, bringing its determining influence to bear .... It can neither be foreseen nor calculated, neither counted nor measured. The wish of "good luck" which people give one another at each new undertaking, and which reveals their belief in a metaphysical factor operating in economic life, is nothing other than the secular translation of *Hashem's* blessing. (*The Call of the Torah*, p. 664)

Evidence of an "immaterial factor" that can be neither "foreseen nor calculated" supplies a basis for the contention that world events are a mask for the will of *Hashem*. He can turn the heart of a tyrant or orchestrate an otherwise minor event that alters the larger course of history. This is the foundation of faith. And this faith affords the Jewish people—so painfully buffeted by the perils of *galus* (exile)—great peace of mind. As the Chazon Ish states in his *Emunah Uvitachon*:

When confronted with an occurrence in which, according to the way of the world, danger lies ahead, it is natural to become frightened. Melancholy causes one to forget that occurrences have no mastery over us, for nothing can restrain *Hashem* from sending salvation and from setting in motion causes which will overturn the apparent conclusion. Forbearance in such difficult moments is instilling in oneself the known truth that no harmful occurrence is left to chance, for everything is from *Hashem*, whether good or the opposite; when the essence of one's *emunah* drives away all fear and gives one the strength to believe that rescue is a possibility—this is *bitachon*.

In the *Divine* scheme of things, "occurrences have no mastery over us ...." The outcome is solely in the hands of our Creator. This most comforting belief is, indeed, the true purpose of studying history.

"Remember the history (lit., 'days') of the world, understand the years of generation upon generation." (*Devarim* 32:7)

Rabbi Shlomo Rottenberg elucidates this verse in *Am Olam*:

"... Precisely through the remembrance of *Yemos Olam* (the history of the world), with their constant march of mighty feats and Divine Providence, man learns to know his Creator."[8]

Studying history, in the Torah perspective, is not mere "longing for the good old days" or a morbid fascination with what once was, but nothing less than the search for *Hashem*. Recognizing *Hashem's* Presence in history strengthens our *emunah* that He is with us now, no less than in the past.

• Themes of the Century

Deciding how to present the events raised some questions: Should the events be presented in the order in which they occurred? Or should they be rearranged according to common theme? What is the "common theme" of a given event? Are there common themes in events that cover an entire century? How many common themes are there?

For various reasons, the "general themes" presentation was chosen, and therefore, events are sorted into sections, each beginning with an explanatory overview.

When viewed as a whole, analysis of these events yielded four major themes:

1. *In Hashem's Hands:*
   We discuss several major battles of World War II containing unpredictable elements of *hashgachah* or "luck," upon which these battles, and ultimately the war, hinged.[9]

2. *Smashing Strange Idols:*
   We delve into prominent events of the twentieth century

espousing anti- or non-Torah ideologies, which, despite their widespread popularity, proved as bankrupt as the stone or wooden idols of the ancient world.

3. *Smashing the Idols of Technology*:
We examine some of the breathtaking advances in science in the twentieth century to alert us to the dangers of over-reliance upon technology.

4. *Portents of Armageddon*:

We address a unique and frightening development of the modern era: the prospect of global annihilation through nuclear warfare. We present a Torah perspective to help deal with the terrifying possibilities.

Since history is not easily classified into neat little categories, some events may not fit perfectly into their categories. This arrangement is intended to provide readers a conceptual scaffold with which they may gain greater understanding of what might be happening "behind the scenes."

ACKNOWLEDGMENTS

This book is first and foremost dedicated to my father. Among his many outstanding attributes, he was a master storyteller. I don't know if he was naturally born with the ability or he perfected it through practice—probably both—but whether in person or on a public stage, he always had a story to tell that was sure to touch the heart. At the same time, in addition to his story-telling prowess, he loved history. No era or aspect of history was foreign to him. He was particularly fascinated by World War II. The reader will quickly see that this, too, is one of my pet subjects. This book, then, is more than dedicated to him. It is, in so many ways, an extension of him. If you find value in this book, it is because of him.

As *hashgachah* would have it, this book is currently scheduled to be published on or around his third *yahrtzeit*, 15 Elul 5707. I am humbled at the thought. May his memory be a blessing.

Many other people helped round this book into what it is. Nachum Shapiro, Managing Editor at Judaica Press, was on board with the project from the very beginning. He was the first to tell me that I had a book and supplied early guidance on how best to conceive and organize it.

At one point, I felt too overwhelmed with other obligations to follow through on this project. Rabbi Moshe Weinberger, who in many ways became like a second father to me, is the one who encouraged me to break through whatever obstacles I thought were in the way and just start writing it. Thank you, Rabbi Weinberger, for your inspiration and encouragement.

Rabbi Nissan Wolpin, Editor of *The Jewish Observer*, was the first to publish an article of mine on history and *hashgachah* (much of which became the chapter on D-Day in this book). That was almost two decades ago and his faith in me has shaped much of my writing confidence and style since then.

Rabbi Pinchas Lipschutz, Editor of *Yated Ne'eman*, published many of my articles on history and *hashgachah*. Often his feedback, or the feedback of one of his editors, or even one of his readers, helped me sharpen and clarify passages in this book.

Recently, I worked with Rabbi Joseph Elias on a Holocaust Curriculum guide for Torah Umesorah. In addition to Lesson Plans, the guide includes supplemental readings for the students. Some of the supplemental material included selections from chapters that would eventually become this book. Although Rabbi Elias did not read them with full scrutiny for final editing purposes, he often provided a perspective that enhanced mine and/or offered a comment that led me to revise and improve the draft. Similarly, at one point, Rabbi Nosson Scherman of Artscroll reviewed the Holocaust Curriculum and a few of his comments on what became part of this book enabled me to improve the draft. Let me be clear that neither rabbi read the full manuscript of this book, nor even the majority of it. However, the comments on the parts they did read were valuable.

Rabbi Yonason Rosenblum and Rabbi Yitzchak Adlerstein took time from extremely busy schedules to make much-appreciated critiques and/or comments on parts of an early draft.

Rabbi Shraga Feivel Zimmerman, whose rabbinic guidance and keen insight into life issues has enriched me immeasurably, read through the entire manuscript and made extremely valuable suggestions.

Rabbi Ephraim Oratz went through the entire manuscript, too, and provided a list of worthy suggestions that were incorporated into the final product.

Mrs. Toby Cohen edited the final draft and fine-tuned it with her sharp editorial skills. She not only improved the writing but raised issues that led to changes that improved the structure and content of the book.

The staff at Judaica Press has done a fantastic job designing the book and especially the cover. They even came up with the title, which, alas, to my chagrin, I did not have the merit to think up. Although my ego initially had a hard time admitting that someone else had come up with a better title than mine, it was quickly obvious to me that, dare I say, their title seemed Divinely inspired. Indeed, one could say a "hidden hand" was at work through the staff at Judaica Press to come up with the title of this book.

Lastly, I want to thank my *aishes chayil* and children for, among other things, their role in the creation of this book. It's not always easy being the spouse or child of a writer. Writing is a generally solitary process. Loved ones need to give the writer in their life space at times. I thank them for their understanding and patience in this area. You all give me life, pleasure, happiness and *brachah*.

What would a book about the "Hidden Hand" of *Hashem* in history be if it did not conclude with an acknowledgment of the One whose Hand is eminently and continually operating in our lives? Tying the circle together, I thank *Hashem* for bringing me into this world through loving parents, including a gifted father with a penchant for storytelling and history, and endowing me with abilities, people and circumstances that have allowed this book to come to fruition.

In Hashem's Hands

OVERVIEW

"Precisely through the remembrance of Yemos
Olam *(the history of the world), with their
constant march of mighty feats and Divine Providence,
man learns to know his Creator."*

—AM OLAM, BY RABBI SHLOMO ROTTENBERG

The first principle of Judaism is recognition of an existing, all-powerful, all-knowing G-d, who directs the course of events, large and small.[10] This is the meaning of the First Commandment:

"I am *Hashem*, your G-d, who took you out of the land of Egypt, the house of bondage." (*Shemos* 20:2)

Why does *Hashem* identify Himself "merely" as the G-d who took the Jews out of Egypt? True, the *Makkos* (Ten Plagues) and *Kriyas Yam Suf* (the Splitting of the Red Sea) were unparalleled miracles. But do they compare to the act of creating the universe? Would it not make more of an impression to define Himself as the "Creator of Heaven and Earth"?

However, by describing Himself as the G-d who just took the Jews out of slavery, *Hashem* focuses on the key defining quality of His revealed Self: His involvement with humans. He is not just the G-d of creation, but He cares about His creations: He is the G-d of history. He is not the stoic "Unmoved Mover" described in Greek philosophy. He is not the faceless, aloof G-d of the Deist. He is *intensely interested* in human affairs, and He "came down" into the Land of Egypt to free His people "from the house of bondage."

The first of the Ten Commandments teaches, therefore, that

Hashem created the universe long ago, and remains intimately involved in its affairs, i.e., that of human beings. He did not just ignite a "Big Bang" long ago, and leave a universe on its own to run like clockwork (as fancied by the ancient Greeks and modern Deists). Rather, He cares and is concerned. He *is* Care and Concern. He is "mindful" of humanity. Human beings mean something to Him.[11]

This is the quintessential principle of the Torah's perspective on history: There is a G-d *who is involved in world events.*

✦ ✦ ✦

Dovid Hamelech (King David), who among many other things was a warrior of legendary stature, wrote: "These [put their faith] in horses, and those in chariots, but we [pray to] the Name of our G-d." (*Tehillim* 20:8)

His son, Shlomo Hamelech (King Solomon)—wisest of the wise—wrote: "The heart of a king is like streams of water in the hand of *Hashem*. He directs it wherever He wishes." (*Mishlei* 21:1)

These and other Torah passages invoking *yad Hashem* (the "hand of *Hashem*") find support in the battles and wars fought in the "bloody twentieth" century. This is quite surprising, since technology had advanced the "art of war" to a degree unimaginable to earlier generations, which one would have thought would have produced complete control over the outcome. However, this was not so. Time and again, the most important military moments hinged on an unplanned, inexplicable, unavoidable simple twist of fate—the element we call *hashgachah* (Divine Providence).

In our morning prayers, we describe *Hashem* as "*Baal Hamilchamos*," "Master of War." This means that He has complete mastery over even the seeming chaos of war. The enemy may have horses and chariots—or tanks and bombs—but we have *bitachon* (faith/trust) that these are not the determining factors. The outcome is in His hands.

✦ ✦ ✦

The common denominator of the incidents in this section is to reveal how miracles—even minor ones—still occur, even in modern times. The most ardent secularists admit how dumbfounded they are by the little coincidences that turned victory to defeat, or defeat to victory. Indeed, as we delve "behind the scenes," we will find, time and again, pivotal moments turning on the most improbable circumstances. This study confirms what the wisest of men said long ago:

The heart of the king is in the hand of Hashem ....

The Miracle
of Dunkirk

A group of British soldiers arrives in England after the evacuation of Flanders, France, on June 6, 1940, in World War II. The British soldier at left wears his pajamas instead of his uniform and a blanket around his shoulders for warmth, and smokes a pipe. In Operation Dynamo, over three hundred thousand French, British and Belgian troops escaped the German invasion from the beaches near Dunkirk, France. (AP Photo)

"Suddenly the scene has cleared, the crash
and thunder has for the moment—but only
for the moment—died away. A miracle of
deliverance is manifest to us all."

(WINSTON CHURCHILL ~ JUNE 4, 1940)

It is 5:30 A.M., May 10, 1940. The world stands on edge. The two largest, most advanced armies ever assembled are about to face off against each other: Germany in the East vs. France and Britain in the West. The tense months since the defeat of Poland in September 1939 are about to come to a crashing end.

Germany's decisive military victories in Poland and Norway had forced France and Britain to declare war against her, but they had not yet launched a significant attack. During the following winter and spring, these two Allies began concentrating troops along the Maginot Line, a series of underground concrete fortifications stretching eighty-seven miles, with tank obstacles, machine gun posts and heavy artillery guns built into the hills bordering France and Germany. Hundreds of feet below these hills, half a million French and British soldiers lay in wait, primed and ready to take on the German onslaught.

The Maginot forts were indeed a twentieth century wonder. Advanced elevator systems brought stores of ammunition directly up to the guns ready to be continually reloaded. Electric trains underground moved troops with ease from barracks to battle stations. The troops waiting out the long, winter months of this "Phony War," as it became termed, entertained themselves in cinemas, sunray rooms and other accoutrements in their air-conditioned underground home-away-from-home.

The Maginot Line, nicknamed the "Shield of France," was one

The Miracle of Dunkirk

reason the Allies were certain of trouncing their enemy. More so, the Allies had a larger army (152 divisions vs. 135 for Germany), and many more tanks (4,204 to 2,493), artillery guns (13,974 to 7,378) and aircraft (4,981 to 3,369) than the Germans. Another advantage was the expertise of the French, who had helped introduce the tank and the airplane in World War I, and whose newer, improved tanks were superior to the Germans'. Joining the French were 200,000 highly skilled soldiers of the British Expeditionary Forces (BEF).

Clearly, they had much to rely on. Germany's easy victory over Poland was the natural result of a modern army attacking an ill-equipped second-rate army still using horses against tanks! Now Germany faced an army "up to its weight," and the Allies' confidence seemed warranted.

✦ *However, as King David warns against relying upon "chariot and horse," an Almighty G-d runs Heaven and Earth, and only His will matters. If He so chooses, He may put a thought into one leader or general's mind, and withhold an important thought from the opposing leader or general's mind.*

• Blitzkrieg

When Hitler came to power in 1933, Winston Churchill notably commented, "Thank G-d for the French Army."

His dependence, however, was misplaced. France had long ceased to uphold their renown as military giant of Europe. The French had rested too long upon their laurels, and now suffered from the "affliction" of victory. French military manuals still devoted page after page to the tactics of the First World War. There was no attempt to upgrade old methods. France had pioneered motor transport in warfare, but had reverted to relying on railway and the horse. France could deploy 1,000 tanks more than the Germans, but continued to arrange them in small, tightly controlled battalions to support the infantry. This handicapped them to maintaining the same 3 mph speed of infantry troops since the times of Alexander.

In contrast, the Germans would unleash a radically new military strategy, the Blitzkrieg, or "Lightning War." Their strategy worked by dispatching tanks to lead the attack, followed by the infantry, for mopping-up and filling the gaping holes of destruction left by the rampaging tanks. This new use of the tank, in coordination with other modern advancements such as the airplane and radio, created a fast-paced, chaotic battlefield, something the French Army was ill-suited and untrained for.

The vaunted Maginot Line proved to be the greatest liability of all in this new world of mobile warfare.[12] First, it lulled the French into a false sense of security. Second, this security caused them to ignore other areas and strategies for defense, most importantly, the Ardennes Forest. The eighty-seven fortified miles of the Maginot Line stopped at the Ardennes, whose two hundred miles of thick woods and winding, narrow pathways were considered impenetrable.[13] The French had stationed only a small portion of ill-trained and poorly equipped divisions there.

• The Sickle Cut

The Germans called their invasion plan *"Sichelschnitt"* ("Sickle Cut"), as it aimed to slice through the Ardennes Forest and come down behind the Maginot Line, effectively surrounding the Allied forces.

One of Germany's leading generals had contended that the Ardennes could be traversed quickly by tank, and eventually his view won the day. The German strategists then set up a cunning, three-fold plan. First, they positioned a relatively small decoy force opposite the Maginot Line, effectively eliminating the half million French soldiers who stood poised inside the forts, waiting for an attack that never came.

Second, to divert attention away from activity in the Ardennes Forest, a significant German army force invaded Belgium and the Netherlands (the "Low Countries"), north of the forest. However, the main attack—Part Three—was directly through the heart of the Ardennes Forest, which lay between the "Low Countries" and the French defenses at the Maginot Line.

On May 10, long columns of German tanks, stretching as much as 100 miles, entered the Ardennes unnoticed. While they embarked upon a two to three day journey through the winding roads, a second German army attacked Holland and Belgium. Assuming that this was the main attack, 400,000 top French and British divisions moved into Belgium to confront the aggressors.

Suddenly, three days into the battle—May 13—seemingly from out of nowhere, columns of speeding German tanks burst out of the "impenetrable" Ardennes Forest. Virtually unopposed, they sliced through the soft, unprotected underbelly of the French defenses behind the lines of those fighting in Belgium. The Allies had been lured straight into the trap Hitler and his generals had set for them.

As the charging Nazi Panzer divisions swept north, they cut—as a sickle—French and British soldiers in Belgium from their forces and supplies line back in France. The French had no plan for a counterattack and fell into disarray. General Maurice Gamelin, their Supreme Commander, was old and out of touch, and uninformed of the calamity in time.[14] By May 20, he was fired and replaced.

By May 24, a mere two weeks into the war, the Germans had cornered the French and British armies into an ever-shrinking pocket along the beaches of the French coastal town of Dunkirk.[15]

"Nothing but a miracle can save the BEF now," said General Alan Brooke, one of the British commanders trapped in France.[16]

The question was how many Allied soldiers could be evacuated to England before their resistance was crushed. "We shall have lost practically all our trained soldiers in the next few days—unless a miracle appears to help us," wrote General Edmund Ironside, Chief of the Imperial General Staff.[17]

In England, newly appointed Prime Minister Winston Churchill[18] was not optimistic and warned the House of Commons to expect "hard and heavy tidings."

However, "the heart of the king is in the hand of *Hashem*" (*Mishlei* 21:1). Just when things looked bleakest, the Creator of Heaven and Earth put a thought into the one man who could alter the course of history for the Nazis. That man was Adolf Hitler.

• The Miracle

On May 24, Hitler suddenly gave orders to halt the relentless onslaught. This was almost inexplicable.[19] Various reasons were given for the decision, such as bestowing upon his friend Hermann Goering, Commander of the Luftwaffe (Nazi Air Force), the "honor" of finishing off the beleaguered troops.[20] Whatever the idea was that fell into his mind—and produced that memorable order—it saved the lives of the Allied troops, and also proved to be one of the turning points of the war.

As early as May 22, preparations were underway for the evacuation (code-named "Operation Dynamo") of the 200,000 British and 160,000 French soldiers, largely unarmed (they had been forced to leave behind all heavy artillery and equipment), and helplessly awaiting their fate on the beaches of Dunkirk. Churchill later said he hadn't expected more than 20,000 to 30,000 men to be evacuated safely. Initially, before the Führer halted his tanks, the goal for British Naval ships was to recover 45,000 men of the British Expeditionary Force over a period of two days. That was soon expanded to include 120,000 men over five days. On the evening of May 26, the first troops evacuated numbered 8,000.

Since the entire British Navy was not large enough to evacuate all the men, a call went out to civilians with seaworthy vessels to help in the rescue. A vast armada of boats large and small, fishing boats and pleasure craft from dozens of coastal holiday resorts answered the call and, captained by elderly and teenaged owners, ceaselessly crossed and recrossed the English Channel for days, rescuing the besieged troops. Many were sunk, and hundreds of soldiers and rescuers were killed by the relentless Luftwaffe, strafing and shelling the Channel and the beaches of Dunkirk.

By May 31, the pocket had shrunk down to an area little more than a couple of square miles. But, soldier by soldier, they made it off the doomed beachhead, and by June 4, after only nine days, an incredible total of 338,226 troops had been evacuated aboard some 700 different vessels![21]

Churchill himself referred to the operation as a "miracle."[22] And, indeed, it was. A great calamity had been reversed— "Remember Dunkirk"—to a virtual victory, because those 300,000 soldiers lived to fight another day, later serving as backbone forces in the defense of Britain and in the ultimate victory of the Allies over the Nazis. The foundation for final victory had surely been laid in Dunkirk.

° An Oasis in the Desert of *Din*

Thus far history. The deeper story and the Torah lessons therein far transcend the events themselves.

Of course, the "Miracle of Dunkirk" notwithstanding, the Battle of France was a resounding defeat for the Allies, and especially for Jews. First, thousands of Jewish refugees from Germany, Austria and Czechoslovakia were now trapped behind German lines in Holland and Belgium. Also, Germany had essentially eliminated its main threat in Europe, which made it free to concentrate on its diabolical Final Solution of a "Judenrein" Europe.

May 10, 1940, fell on the second day of Iyar. 2 Iyar, according to some opinions, is the day Rabbi Akiva's 24,000 *talmidim* (students) began dying, and thus many Jews begin observing the mourning period (not shaving, no music, etc.) from that day.

Also, in that very month of May/Iyar, the Jews in Krakow and other Polish cities were first deported eastward. More ominously, on May 20 of that very year, as the Allied armies crumbled almost overnight, a concentration camp began functioning in Poland. It's name: Auschwitz.

The month of Iyar, as a prelude to *Matan Torah* (the giving of the Torah), has historically been a time of some of the most devastating tragedies for the Jewish people, starting with the deaths of Rabbi Akiva's 24,000 students and continuing through the Crusades, when Jews throughout Europe were murdered by the thousands.[23]

Iyar is a time of *din*, judgment. *Din* implies that every inner thought, outer behavior or errant word is potentially judged by the strictest standards. However, as the Rashi in *Bereishis* tells us, the world cannot—and was not meant to—exist on strict judgment alone. Iyar is preceded by Nisan, the month of redemption from Egypt, a time of Divine Mercy, when *B'nei Yisrael* (the Jewish people) were taken out of bondage even though we had fallen to the 49th level of *tumah*, of defilement, and even though there were among us people who worshipped idols. Nisan is the month of *chessed*, of kindness and mercy. Our sins are diminished, if not entirely overlooked.

The *chessed* of Nisan is followed by the *gevurah* (strict judgment) of Iyar. However, even within the strict judgment of Iyar, there's slight reprieve, a sweetening of the bitterness, called *Lag B'Omer*, the 33rd day of the Omer, a day when Rabbi Akiva's students did not die.

No one can survive total, absolute judgment. Indeed, *Hashem* is ultimately the *Av Harachamim*, the Father of Mercy.[24] He does not want our death or suffering (although we must be prepared to accept the fact that either or both may be a part of His plan in the overall picture). So He gives us a *Lag B'Omer* to remind us that strict judgment is not the be-all, end-all of His relationship with us. His true goal is *gilui haShechinah*, the revelation of His very Self at *Har Sinai*. That's where we are headed; that's what our counting is about. The judgment is a necessary component of our improvement, a disciplinary aid that will lead to our ultimate completeness, our ability to absorb Truth.

Lag B'Omer is an oasis in the desert of *din*. It's a reminder that there is life even in the driest, most barren desert; hope, even in the most painful suffering; light, even in the deepest darkness.

Bearing this in mind—and bearing in mind that if we observe in the history of events something that we feel points to *hashgachah*, nevertheless common sense and humility compel us to describe it as merely a possibility and suggestion—there is a fascinating footnote to this chapter in the history of World War II.

Lag B'Omer 5700 coincided with May 26, 1940, the day subsequent history would mark as the beginning of the "Miracle of Dunkirk," the day the first group of a defeated remnant of Allied soldiers was miraculously rescued, and lived to fight another day!

It seems as if the month of *din* (i.e., Iyar) challenges our *emunah* with horrific instances of seeming randomness, of *tzaddik v'ra lo*, "bad things happening to good people." And perhaps this is necessary as we draw nearer to the truth—to *Matan Torah*— to the truth that there are no random events; that *Hashem* runs the world.

And yet—it seems that there must always be that oasis in the desert of *din*, *Lag B'Omer*. It is almost as if the message of *Lag B'Omer* was being broadcast through the events themselves. An oasis of redemption stood out in a desert of death; a ray of light shone brightly even as the night of Nazi darkness fell all around— a ray that would eventually overcome and overwhelm the darkness.

The Battle
of Britain

The burned-out wrecks of London taxicabs in Leicester Square
reflect the damage done by the German firebombing night raids
on Britain's capital, November 8, 1940. (AP Photo)

*"Never in the field of human conflict was
so much owed by so many to so few."*

(Winston Churchill)

"The final German victory over England is now only a question of time," General Alfred Jodl, Hitler's right-hand man, wrote on June 30, 1940.

The Germans had overrun Belgium, the Netherlands and northern France by the end of May 1940. Russia would not enter the war against Germany until June 1941, nor the United States until December of that year. Britain was alone and helpless.

The Germans' strategy for the invasion of England—an operation code-named "Sea Lion"—was to first win air superiority over Britain. Therefore, less than three weeks after the fall of France, Field Marshall Hermann Goering, head of the Luftwaffe, ordered his forces to draw the RAF into battle and destroy them. He was confident of the outcome, since Germany's air force out-numbered Britain's by nearly four-to-one, a force of 1,300 bombers, 760 fighter planes and 300 dive-bombers.

Though badly outnumbered, the British had one distinct advantage: a brand new technology called radar.[25] The moment a squadron of German planes took off from their base in Western Europe, it was spotted on British radar screens, its course accurately plotted. This was something new in warfare, and it puzzled the Germans, who were far behind the British in the development and use of this electronic device.

Yet, even with radar, the British were floundering. Wave upon wave of Nazi bombers and fighters, usually three tiers thick, attacked convoys in the English Channel, as well as airfields and the vital radar stations on the ground, intending to deal a deathblow to the RAF. The British pilots fought bravely from the beginning. But in mid-August, the Luftwaffe stepped up their attacks, hammering at England's most strategic targets. The RAF was wearing down, and actually running out of pilots.[26] They even began training eighteen-year-olds and sending them into combat after an inadequately short, ten-hour training period. Many of these pilots died before they learned how to fight. As August progressed, Goering was confident enough to assure Hitler that a few more days of concentrated attacks on the RAF would enable operation "Sea Lion" to proceed.

• Enter "Fate"

Then, just when things looked most bleak, a "twist of fate" changed the course of the battle—and history.

The Luftwaffe's orders were expressly to destroy military bases and arsenals, but to avoid bombing London for fear of retaliatory strikes on German cities. However, one night (August 24), a fleet of German bombers lost their way. Unaware that they were directly over London, they dropped their bombs, blowing up homes and killing civilians. The outraged British retaliated the very next evening, sending a squadron of bombers over Berlin.

While only about half of the eighty-one RAF bombers found their targets that night, and not one Berliner was killed, the raid's effect on the German psyche was devastating. Goering had unabashedly promised the German people that bombs would never fall on Berlin.[27] Now, the unthinkable had happened. The German capital *had* been attacked.

The furious Nazi leader did not immediately retaliate, but after the RAF bombers had hit Berlin four more times,[28] Hitler finally changed his policy. Rather than continuing to pound military targets, he would attack civilian ones. He announced his plans to his nation on September 4: "When the British Air Force drops two or three or four thousand kilograms of bombs," the Nazi warlord shouted angrily, as he waved his hands and stomped up and down, "then we will—in one night!—drop 150-, 230-, 300- or 400,000 kilograms .... When they declare that they will increase their attacks on our cities, then we will raze their cities to the ground!"

This pronouncement received thunderous applause, but the decision cost him the Battle of Britain, and ultimately, the war.

The bombardment of Britain began on September 7, with the Luftwaffe deploying over a thousand planes—625 bombers and 648 fighters—over London. They flew over the Thames River (which runs through the heart of London), dropping their munitions. Hundreds were killed, thousands injured and tens of thousands rendered homeless.[29] Entire blocks of the British capital became a single mass of flames. The assault continued for a terrible fifty-seven consecutive nights—an average of two hundred bombers per raid.[30]

Despite the onslaught, the British "stiff upper lip" remained firm. The more London burned, the greater grew their resolve. Images of families and entire neighborhoods huddled together on cots, underground in subways, always making the best of the situation, graced newspapers and newsreels, creating the legend of "The Battle of Britain."[31]

Yet, despite the great terror and slaughter of civilians, and destruction of docks, railways and factories, this shift in German strategy had bought the RAF crucial breathing space. While the Luftwaffe focused its attacks on London and its citizens, the RAF was able to fill in the holes on its airfields, repair equipment, reconnect the communications and gather its breath. British aircraft factories were able to continue production.[32] Attacking British civilians assuaged the Nazis' rage, but it ruined their chance of winning the Battle of Britain[33]—and in retrospect, the entire war. It was a fatal mistake.[34]

• The Chess Master

Secular historians often employ the terms "ill-luck" or "pure chance" to describe events such as the one that led Nazi bombers astray, causing them to bomb London and change the course of the war. However, the Torah perspective understands that the hand of *Hashem* is what moves the "players" on the "playing field," not instrument panels or map readings.

An event in *parashas* (the weekly Torah portion of) *Beshalach* drives home this point. The beginning of this *parashah* describes how *Hashem* lured the Egyptian army into the *Yam Suf* and then destroyed them. Here, *Hashem* commands Moshe to tell the people to stand back and let the hand of *Hashem* perform the miraculous.

The end of the *parashah* describes the war with Amalek, a war fought with soldiers and swords, a "natural," non-miraculous war. Nevertheless, following this battle, Moshe builds an altar and calls it "*Hashem* is my banner." (*Shemos* 17:15)

He did this, Rashi explains, to offset any possibility in their minds that the victory came through their own power rather than the hand of *Hashem*. The *parashah* concludes (v. 16): "*Hashem* will be at war with Amalek forever." The *Kesav Sofer* comments, "Know this rule forever: When the Jewish people gain victory over their enemies by the sword, it is not through their own power. Rather, '*Hashem* is their banner.' It is He who brings us victory."[35]

The perfect symmetry of these two very different-looking wars teaches us the Torah's viewpoint on war. Whether overtly miraculous or not, the same "hand of *Hashem*" is at work, steering the king, his advisors, soldiers[36] and people wherever He wants.

"The Battle of Britain," a remarkable contemporary example of such an occurrence, embodies King Solomon's teaching:

"The heart of the king is in the hand of G-d; He turns it wherever He wants."

The king is typically the most powerful person in the land. No one tells him what to do. He commands generals, ministers, counselors and politicians. Yet, the wisest of men, himself a king, said, "The king's heart is in the hand of G-d." Even when the king thinks he's acting on his own, *Hashem* directs his heart like a stream, turning it wherever He wants.

Rabbi Shlomo Rottenberg (*Am Olam*) compares *Hashem's* manipulation of the king's heart to the movement of chess pieces on a chessboard. "Their king," he says, "really is no king, their queen is no queen, and their knights are not knights. There is a Divine Hand that moves the pieces to their required positions. For they and their hearts are but in His Hand—to be led to victory or defeat."

This dynamic is evident most poignantly in the actions of Adolf Hitler, the only flesh-and-blood creature on the planet that could have slowed or stopped the Nazi onslaught on England. Had he pressed the RAF and its infrastructure for another week or two, it might never have recovered. But at the key moment, his heart was manipulated, as was Pharaoh's:

"I will harden Pharaoh's heart ...." (*Shemos* 14:4)

The "Chess Master" moved the pawn known as *der Führer's* heart, and the course of the war—indeed, history—was changed forever.

Day of Infamy

U.S. President Franklin D. Roosevelt signs the declaration of war following the
Japanese bombing of Pearl Harbor, Dec. 7, at the White House in Washington, D.C.,
December 8, 1941, at 3:08 MJ. EST. (AP Photo)

"December 7, 1941—a date which lives in infamy"

FRANKLIN D. ROOSEVELT

It is **December 7, 1941**, one week before *Chanukah* (Hanukkah). Hitler's armies are only twenty miles from the Kremlin, and German soldiers are even joking about catching a bus to visit Stalin.

Stalin is no friend of the Jews, but nevertheless, he is vital to the fate of Jewry, as well as the world. For if the Soviet capital falls, Germany need not fear a two-front war. If the German armies are able to gather all their power and focus on just one front ... the implications are truly frightening to ponder.

It is December 7, 1941, almost dawn. Thousands of miles to the east, somewhere in the middle of the Pacific Ocean, six aircraft carriers have moved into position. On their decks and in their holds, 350 modern fighter aircraft, primed for action, receive the signal: GO! Their target: Pearl Harbor.

At 7:40 A.M., Hawaii Time, the American Pacific Fleet is taken by surprise. In fact, the surprise is so complete that even before the first bomb drops, Squadron Commander Mitsuo Fuchida radios back to the Japanese carriers: Tora! Tora! Tora! (Tiger! Tiger! Tiger!—the code word for victory). In less than three hours, his pilots will wipe out much of the American fleet. Truly, a day of infamy.

✦ ✦ ✦

It is December 7, 1941. In the German-occupied little town of Chelmno, hundreds of miles behind the front lines, scores of unsuspecting Jews are rounded up under the guise that they are merely being relocated east.

The hierarchies of Nazidom have already ordered the "final

solution" to the Jewish question. But, practically speaking, can it be done? Can you get masses of people to walk into a death camp? Can you then exterminate them using a minimum amount of ammunition and soldiers?

Today, they begin their diabolical experiment. The innocent Jewish families are transported to a "resettlement" location in specially made vans—in which all are gassed to death. Today, December 7, 1941, is a particular day of infamy—of the infamy known as the Holocaust—because on this day, the Nazis know that their insidious plan to make Europe *Judenrein* is within their grasp.

Although not until the Wannsee Conference in early 1942 would the bureaucratic wheels be set in motion, and the wheels of cattle cars transporting Jews to death camps would not be rolling for several months, historian Martin Gilbert correctly marks Chelmno as the onset of the Final Solution.

Truly, a day that will live forever in infamy.

• Of Historical Moments

We are helpless, hapless creatures in the absence of Divine perspective. Our helplessness is even more pronounced during momentous events. Most people are impotent to realize what is happening. And the few who do realize are at a loss to understand. The rare individual who understands a historic moment as it occurs will still be lacking some details to comprehend all the implications.

When divergent threads of historical movement converge into a single moment, such as on December 7, 1941, Judaism calls it *hashgachah*—"Divine Providence": the acknowledgment that everything happens because a Master Weaver is expertly spinning a perfectly patterned tapestry. Sometimes, the pattern is not immediately apparent. But we, who know the Weaver, have faith that the final design will be awe-inspiringly visible, clear and true.

Unfortunately, we often shy away from invoking the term "Divine Providence" when events work against us. Yet, if *Hashem* can manipulate events for our good, does He lose His omnipotence when events work against us? Perceiving Divine Providence on happy occasions is valuable; however, acknowledging Divine Providence with its full effect during difficult and painful events requires a higher level[37] of faith. It requires believing that much more is happening than what meets the eye.

The dark historical moment that was December 7, 1941, which President Roosevelt called "a date which lives in infamy," was actually not completely dark. Like the tiny flask of uncontaminated oil discovered by the *Kohanim* (Jewish priests) on *Chanukah*, it contained within it the most sublime luminescence. Let us observe the inner workings of these three events.

I. General Winter

Hitler's armies were within sight of the Kremlin. In the summer of 1941, German panzers had raced through Russia at breakneck speed, penetrating thousands of square miles into the country. On the first day alone, some 1,200 Russian aircraft had been destroyed, and by nightfall, three infantry divisions (a division consists of 10-20,000 soldiers) had simply vanished! Moscow probably would have been taken in a scant two weeks had the Führer not diverted his armies to other theaters of war that summer. But even so, by December 6, Hitler's seemingly indomitable armies were poised outside the Soviet capital, and on that day the Nazi leader himself boasted: "Today begins the last—the great—battle of this year."

But Hitler had overextended himself. His armies were tired, low on supplies and inadequately clothed for a winter that had set in earlier than usual. It was one of the worst winters in Russian history, and it demoralized the frozen, hungry, frustrated soldiers, whose guns froze and whose tanks wouldn't start. Some German soldiers even prayed that their generals would surrender. The cold worked so well in the Russians' favor that historians credited their victory not to Russia's military genius, but to that ultimate General of all Russian Generals: "General Winter."

The Germans not only failed to gain Moscow, but the Russians successfully counterattacked and gained back some important ground. Most importantly, this date marked a turning point. In the words of William Shirer (*The Rise and Fall of the Third Reich*, p. 865):

> "The myth of the invincibility of the German Army," he [General Franz Halder, Hitler's Chief of Staff] wrote, "was broken." There would be other German victories in Russia when another summer came around, but they could never restore the myth. December 6, 1941 is another turning point in the short history of the Third Reich and one of the most fateful ones. Hitler's power had reached its zenith; from now on, it was to decline, sapped by the growing counterblows of the nations against which he had chosen to make aggressive war."

The war was three and a half years from its end, but already on December 7, 1941, the pendulum had swung, imperceptibly perhaps, but undeniably away from the Nazis, and they would never recover.

II. The Sleeping Giant

Thousands of miles away, over the warm skies of Hawaii, Japanese squadron leader Fuchida had returned safely to his carrier and awaited the signal from fleet commander Vice Admiral Chuichi Nagumo to renew the attack. Dockyard installations and oil stores in Pearl Harbor were still largely intact. And the U.S. aircraft carriers, the primary targets of the mission, had not been hit or even discovered yet.

Fuchida waited ... and waited. The signal never came. Nagumo's decision to return to Tokyo without delivering the real deathblow is something historians still debate and wonder about to this day.

But America, the invincible giant, had been toppled, its aura of impregnability violated. Panic struck the hearts of American citizens, especially in California, where all were convinced a Japanese invasion would take place the next day. The government rashly ordered the interment to special camps of all American citizens of Japanese descent. (No such actions were taken against Americans of German or Italian ancestry.)

America had been rocked and badly shaken. But with the clarity of backward vision, we see what a G-dsend that dose of reality was. It awakened a sleeping giant. That giant now joined a war it had heretofore shunned. Once aroused, America flung all its industrial and economic power into action, and forever changed the destiny of World War II. Thus, with perfect hindsight, all can plainly see how the tragedy of December 7, 1941, in Pearl Harbor was necessary to ensure victory for the free world, including the remnant of Israel.

III. The Final Solution & the Final Redemption

Of the fateful events of December 7, 1941, the tragedy of Chelmno—which set in motion the annihilation of six million Jews—must also have somehow harbored seeds of redemption. It is perhaps presumptuous to even suggest that this darkest event could contain light, but our Faith tells us it must be so.

Some people say, "Look, the fact is that right after the Holocaust we regained control over *Eretz Yisrael* (the land of Israel)." And it is not unreasonable to suggest that world opinion, including the U.N.'s, which granted Israel its nationhood, would not have swung to the side of the Jews if not for the collective pity and/or guilt that the Holocaust produced.

Others say, "The Holocaust, for better or worse, became the only connection many Jews had to Judaism." This, too, is true. For many, it became the anchor of Jewish identity in the decades after the Holocaust, even to this day.

Still others contend, "The entire *Baal Teshuva* (Jews returning to Torah observance) movement would not have come about had not the recent past shocked and awakened many of us into re-examining who we are."

But, in a way, all these and other reasons seem cheap. We are not to comfort a mourner before his loved one is buried, while the wound is still fresh, the Talmud teaches. Many people still feel the wound very deeply. While survivors and their children still breathe, can we really say anything is compensation? Perhaps we as a collective entity are just not ready.

• The Mission of Evil

When we accept the concept of *hashgachah*, we understand the deep truth that there is no reality other than *Hashem*. "Everything *Hashem* does is good." The power of evil is an illusion.[38] It is merely a pawn in the hands of its Maker.

This lesson is brilliantly illuminated in a Talmudic passage, which originates from an event in the weekly portion read just hours before that day of infamy back in 1941.

Parashas Vayishlach recounts the incident where Yaakov meets up with a "man" on the eve before he confronts his murderous brother Esav and a horde of several hundred mercenary soldiers. This man, *Chazal* (the Sages) tell us, was really the angel of Esav, the angel of evil. Yaakov and the angel begin wrestling with each other. The scuffle continues through night, until Yaakov finally begins to prevail. At dawn, the angel says, "Let me go, for dawn is breaking." Rashi (drawing on *Chullin* 91b) explains: "For dawn is breaking and I must sing songs [to *Hashem*]." But Yaakov does not let him go, and asks the angel its name. It replies: "Henceforth, you will be called *Yisrael*, for you have fought with [an angel of] *Hashem* and man, and have prevailed."

Rabbi Moshe Weinberger explains this strange passage with an analogy: Imagine the town bully confronts you in a dark alley. Nowhere else to run, you fight back. Not only do you hold him off, but after a long, bitter fight, you manage to pin him to the concrete! Then, all of a sudden, at that moment, he says, "Oh, I think I hear my mother calling me. Let me go."

That is essentially what happens here. Yaakov, a human being, is confronted by an angel, a divine being. A wrestling match ensues. Yaakov survives, even prevails, and just at the moment of truth, the angel says, "I have to go sing songs to *Hashem*."

a) Why at that moment?

b) How can a flesh and blood creature contend with a divine being?

The explanation is as follows:

An angel is given exactly one mission to perform. As soon as it has completed its task, it goes before *Hashem* and sings songs.

Esav represents evil incarnate. The angel representing him is the source of evil in the world. Evil, however, is not an entity in itself. It is not, as some religions fantasize, an angel that rebelled against *Hashem* and is running loose in the universe. *Evil is a creation of Hashem.* Therefore, evil does not happen if *Hashem* does not want it to happen. If it happens, *Hashem* has a purpose in allowing it to take place.

The angel of Esav, of evil, has one mission, one purpose: *to lose to Yaakov.* That is why, at the precise moment when Yaakov finally and conclusively prevailed over it, the angel of Esav had to return and sing songs before *Hashem*. Its mission had been completed. It had been defeated by good. That is why it was *precisely* at that moment that it had to sing songs before *Hashem*, its Maker.

Evil has no other purpose but to be defeated by good.

The rules have not changed since Yaakov confronted and defeated the angel of Esav/evil. Events that seem to indicate evil's manifest destiny can transform into circumstances of its manifest collapse. And even if the evil proliferates and gains a foothold, its reign is temporary, nothing more than a passing shadow. Evil's dominion is conditional—and always part of a larger picture.

December 7, 1941, was a day of infamy.[39] Yet, at the same time, it contained within it the very elements that would eventually end the immediate infamy. The cure was prepared before the illness, the bandage before the wound. In the end, there is indeed "nothing to fear but fear itself."

Therefore, we have no such thing as a "day of infamy," because there is no infamy. There is only the day, the sowing of a seed of a light that will shine, regardless of the darkness.

The Miracle
at Midway

Smoke burns from the USS *Yorktown* after a Japanese bomber hit the aircraft carrier in the Battle of Midway near Midway Islands in June 1942 during World War II. Bursts from anti-aircraft fire fill the air. (AP Photo/U.S. Navy)

"We had no right to win, when you consider the Japanese force of 185 ships coming against 33 U.S. Navy ships."

(CAPT. STANFORD E. LINZEY JR., A YOUNG SAILOR WHO WAS
PULLED FROM THE WATER AFTER HE AND 2,000 OTHER SAILORS
WERE TOSSED INTO THE SEA WHEN THEIR SHIP SANK,
AND WHO AUTHORED THE BOOK, G-D WAS AT MIDWAY:
THE SINKING OF THE USS YORKTOWN.)

"I have a hunch," Lt. Commander Wade McClusky said as he scanned the vast emptiness of the sparkling blue Pacific from 19,000 feet up.

It was 9:25 A.M. on June 4, 1942.

McClusky, the leader of a formation of dive-bombers from the carrier USS *Enterprise* hunting for a Japanese invasion fleet, had somehow lost track of his fellow squadrons.

Arriving at the reconnaissance spot, they found no one, and their planes were getting low on fuel. Should they turn back or continue? Go north or south?

McClusky, following an irrational "hunch," headed north, which changed not only the course of America's war with Japan in the Pacific, but also the course of the war in Europe.

• The Doolittle Raid

The events leading to McClusky's lucky hunch had begun almost six months earlier, on that "fateful" day, December 7, 1941, when Japan attacked Pearl Harbor. Those early days of 1942 were dark days indeed for America. Day after day, week after week, came news reports of Japanese victories in the Far East. To boost morale, President Roosevelt ordered the "Doolittle Raid."

In April, Lt. Col. James Doolittle led sixteen B-25 bombers on a run over mainland Japan. Some bombers buzzed right over the Imperial Palace of the Emperor himself. The raid caused minimal damage, and no bombs were dropped on the Palace (Doolittle knew from his experiences in London during the Blitz that any serious threat to the Emperor would only stiffen Japanese morale), but it sent shock waves through the Japanese public.

President Roosevelt enigmatically informed reporters that the raid had originated from "Shangri-La," the mysterious Tibetan city from James Hilton's famous novel, *Lost Horizon*. The bombers had actually been launched from the USS *Hornet*, an aircraft carrier stationed several hundred miles east of Japan.[40] The Japanese were certain that large B-25 bombers could not be launched from aircraft carriers, surmising that the attack had come from the nearest American air base, Midway Island, Therefore, they made the decision to invade and capture it.

• David vs. Goliath

Tiny Midway Island, a mere landing strip and base to a few hundred soldiers, lay 1,300 miles west of Pearl Harbor, serving as its early warning outpost. (The Japanese dubbed it "Pearl Harbor's Sentry.") Japan expected that an attack on Midway would lure the American fleet at Pearl Harbor—including the all-important aircraft carriers—to come to its defense, allowing Japan, with its vastly superior numbers, to wipe them out for good. It was a classic David vs. Goliath scenario.

The Japanese had almost 200 ships, including 11 battleships, among which was the most powerful in the world, the *Yamato*, whose eighteen-inch guns were capable of hurling a broadside of more than thirteen tons. Admiral Chuichi Nagumo's First Air Fleet was their main strike force, consisting of seven dangerous aircraft carriers, including the veteran, battle-hardened aircraft carriers *Akagi*, *Kaga*, *Soryu* and *Hiryu*. The Americans were equipped with only thirty-three ships, *none* of which were battleships. Of their three aircraft carriers, the *Yorktown* had been badly damaged in the "Battle of the Coral Sea" a month earlier,[41] and needed three months to be fully repaired. Furthermore, pilots on the *Hornet* had never even flown in battle, compared to the Japanese, who had the world's most-experienced, best-trained pilots.[42]

The Japanese plan seemed like a shoo-in—if they could lure the American fleet into a trap. That trap was Midway.

• The Best-Laid Plans

One factor was to the Americans' advantage: they had broken the Japanese's secret code, and had intercepted radio messages of an imminent attack. They knew the day—June 4—but not the target.

Some strategists suspected Midway, but others disagreed. To confirm their suspicions, they had radio operators on Midway send a phony message to Pearl Harbor that the island was low on vital drinking water due to a breakdown of the water plant. Shortly thereafter, radio operators at Pearl Harbor intercepted a coded Japanese message to Tokyo that the water plant at their intended target was broken. The jubilant Americans now knew the location of the attack—Midway.

Preparations for defense got underway immediately, including a race against time to repair the severely damaged aircraft carrier *Yorktown*. Her flight deck was speedily patched, whole sections of internal beams were cut out and replaced and a new air group was put on her from the naval station's own planes in seventy-two hours![43]

Still, even with three carriers and advance warning, the Americans were seriously outmatched and had no way of knowing from where in the vast ocean the Japanese fleet would arrive. Keeping their spirits up, they code-named the mission "Point Luck."

• The Battle Begins

At 4:30 A.M., June 4, Admiral Nagumo turned his four carriers into the wind, launching more than 100 planes in a two-wave, thirty-one-minute air attack. They inflicted heavy losses upon Midway, but not badly enough to take the island. With its runways damaged but still usable, and some planes still intact, they would have to make a second attack.

Admiral Nagumo was in a quandary. When attacking an island, planes are armed with bombs; but to attack other aircraft carriers, they're armed with torpedoes and other anti-ship weapons. Having planned for only one strike on Midway, his planes were now armed with torpedoes to destroy any U.S. carriers that might arrive from Pearl Harbor. Should he unload the torpedoes for bombs and send a second attack on Midway, or keep the planes loaded with torpedoes in case the enemy suddenly showed up?

Before he could issue orders, bombers from Midway swooped down on his ships. They did no damage, but they made up Nagumo's mind—and changed the course of the battle. He ordered his second-wave torpedo bombers rearmed with bombs for their second attack on Midway.

• The Half-Hour Delay

Thirteen minutes after Admiral Nagumo's orders for the second attack on Midway, a Japanese scout plane radioed in his siting of an American carrier. This plane had taken off that morning *half an hour later than planned, due to a mechanical problem.* Had it taken off on time, it would probably have spotted the U.S. ships half an hour earlier. Nagumo would have then armed his planes with torpedoes and sent them out against the American ships, instead of re-arming them with bombs headed for Midway. Once again, the course of the battle and of the entire Pacific war turned on a simple twist of "fate."

When Nagumo was informed of the carrier's presence, he swiftly ordered the planes to reload with torpedoes. All this took time. In their rush, the ground crews didn't send the unloaded bombs down into the magazine—a protected cavity deep in the ship. Instead, they were stacked on the flight decks alongside the planes, turning the carriers into potential floating infernos—should any aircraft attack them.

• Lost and Confused

At this crucial moment, the American pilots were a confused lot. Since they had left Pearl Harbor, these fighter squadrons and torpedo bombers had been under radio silence, lest the Japanese discover they were on their way. The slow torpedo bombers, flying low, were separated in the clouds from the faster, high-flying, more maneuverable fighter planes sent to protect them.

Disaster struck! The first squadron of American torpedo bombers to find the Japanese was completely wiped out. Not a single torpedo hit its mark. All the pilots except one were killed.[44] The second, and then third squadron of slow torpedo bombers followed, and met a similar fate: no torpedo hits and almost all planes and crewmen lost.

By 10:25 A.M., Admiral Nagumo, anticipating a spectacular victory, ordered his fighter planes out to intercept the American carriers and deliver the killer blow.

• Literally Out of the Blue

In steps Lt. Commander Wade McClusky and his squadron of dive-bombers. Bombers dive at their prey from thousands of feet up high, swooping down at a steep angle before dropping their deadly load, so they literally appeared—out of the blue!

The Japanese couldn't intercept them because their "Zeroes" (fighter planes) were still blowing the American torpedo bombers out of the sky. Thus, all was clear for McClusky's dive-bombers to do their job. Down they plunged, straight at the Japanese carriers with their crammed decks of loosely stacked bombs and planes loaded with explosives and high-octane petrol.

• Five Minutes That Changed History

"The terrifying scream of the dive-bomber reached me first," recalled a Japanese officer from the aircraft carrier *Akagi*, "followed by the crashing explosion of a direct hit. There was a blinding flash and then a second explosion, much louder than the first .... Looking about, I was horrified at the destruction that had been wrought in a matter of seconds. There was a huge hole in the flight deck just behind the amidship elevator. The elevator itself, twisted like molten glass, was drooping into the hangar. Deck plates reeled upward in grotesque configurations. Planes stood tail up, belching livid flame and jet-black smoke."

In five minutes, three Japanese carriers (the *Akagi, Kaga* and *Soryu*) were ablaze, abandoned or crippled. The fourth carrier, *Hiryu*, was originally saved by a squall (sea storm) that suddenly sprang up. It managed to mount a counterattack, its aircraft striking the USS *Yorktown*, which eventually sank. However, by 5 P.M., *Hiryu*, too, was destroyed.

The dreaded Japanese First Air Fleet had been wiped out,[45] and the Japanese never recovered from the devastating losses incurred during the battle of Midway.[46] And what had seemed a perfectly coordinated attack by the Americans had, of course, not been planned at all! The squadrons had been launched in a helter-skelter fashion to begin with,[47] had lost their way and had not been in communication with each other when McClusky's "hunch" brought his planes to "the right place at the right time"!

The American victory at Midway changed not only the course of the war with Japan, but of the war in Europe, too. Had the

Japanese prevailed and captured Midway, and possibly captured Pearl Harbor and destroyed the American fleet, America might have been forced to focus their war effort primarily if not exclusively on Japan. The victory gave Roosevelt the confidence to assure British Prime Minister Winston Churchill that England would no longer fight Hitler alone. The war in Europe would be America's top priority. Thus, much of World War II hinged on those five minutes at Midway. And so much of the "Battle of Midway" hinged on complete "luck."[48]

• Luck? No, Just *Yad Hashem*

Of course, from a Torah standpoint there is no such thing as luck. Luck is another name for *yad Hashem* (the "hand of *Hashem*") subtly intervening in human affairs. Sometimes, our obstacles seem like giants against which we are mere grasshoppers. We feel helpless to stand up to their challenge. And in a world of blind chance, that could be the truth. However, in a world where *yad Hashem* is the operating dynamic, there is no "blind chance."

Yad Hashem doesn't mean that everything will go the way we think it should. It means that behind the "facts" and "factors" of history—large and small, global and personal—the All-Knowing, All-Powerful hand of *Hashem* manipulates events. In a world where *yad Hashem* is hidden, confusing or even seemingly conspiring against us, our task is to peel back the veil, and trust to the depths of our beings that *yad Hashem* is the first and only meaningful rule of history.

The Longest Day

German prisoners of war are led away by Allied forces from Utah Beach on June 6, 1944, during landing operations at the Normandy coast, France. (AP Photo)

*"One night in 1952 during the Presidential campaign,
Dwight Eisenhower confided something to one of
his advisers, a close friend, Senator Frank Carlson.
And Eisenhower told him that during the war
when he was commanding the Allied forces in Europe,
he'd had a startling and vivid spiritual experience—
he had actually felt the hand of G-d guiding him,
felt the presence of G-d ..."*

(PRESIDENT RONALD REAGAN, REMARKS AT THE
ANNUAL NATIONAL PRAYER BREAKFAST, FEBRUARY 6, 1986)

June 6, 1944, is one of the memorable days of the twentieth century. On that day, "D-Day,"[49] the seemingly impregnable armor of Nazi-occupied Europe (sometimes called "Fortress Europe") was pierced.

The largest invasion force ever assembled—6,000 sea vessels, 12,000 planes[50] and 200,000 soldiers—converged on the shores of Normandy, France, all in one long day![51] The invasion was so successful that the combined Allied forces were able to sink a dagger of defeat into the heart of Hitler's "Thousand Year Reich" within one year.[52]

In retrospect, the casual reader of history might believe that such a large invasion could never fail. But on closer inspection, one can perceive that the line between total victory and total defeat was painfully thin. It may seem incomprehensible, but Hitler was just a few simple twists of fate away from eliminating his greatest threat, and tightening his hold on Europe for the unforeseeable future.

• The Sleeping Führer

What was the Nazi Warlord doing that morning?

The Great Dictator was fast asleep. The officer responsible to wake him in case of an emergency convinced himself that the report of Allied attacks in France was not really unusual. In truth, he was terrified to risk stirring the Führer's foul temper. This is the first bit of *hashgachah*.

However, Hitler had a very capable military cabinet. Therefore, at first glance, it may not seem important that he was not immediately informed ... at first glance.

• The Missing General

The most capable of Germany's generals was Erwin Rommel, the famed "Desert Fox," so named for the brilliant victories he had engineered for the Nazis in North Africa. Hitler had put Rommel in charge of fortifying Northern Europe against the anticipated Allied invasion. Experts agree that Rommel's military instinct was the greatest threat to the Allied forces.

Where was Rommel on June 6? After five and a half grueling months in Europe preparing for the anticipated invasion, he decided it was time to pay a visit to the Führer in Germany. Why now? Because Hitler had put the huge division of tanks defending Normandy under his personal command. This worried the "Desert Fox," since, if the invasion were to come, he would need to mobilize the tanks immediately. Waiting for a "go ahead" from the Führer in Berlin could cost him precious hours.

Therefore, on the morning of June 6,

A) Rommel was about 1,000 miles from Normandy,

B) the tank division was still under Hitler's orders, and

C) the Führer, by whose word the tank division could have mobilized to stop the invasion, was fast asleep.[53]

The Crowded Agenda

Obtaining control of the tanks was not Rommel's only reason for leaving the site of the invasion; it may not even have been his main reason. He wanted to return to Germany to get a much-needed rest from the strain of guarding 3,000 miles of European beach.

Also, weather reports predicted a continuation of the gales and storms that were currently besetting northern Europe, which made an invasion highly unlikely at this time.

Furthermore, June 6 was his wife's birthday.

Capricious Weather

The weather also worried General Dwight D. Eisenhower, who headed the Allied invasion forces. In fact, they had actually headed out to sea June 5, only to be called back because of the bad weather. But late on June 5, General Eisenhower received a weather report calling for a partial clearing the next morning—June 6. If Rommel had stayed around a little longer, he might also have received that report.

Eisenhower's decision to move is shrouded in mystery, even to himself.[54] He was aware that weather alone could turn the invasion into the greatest military defeat in history.[55] History is replete with weather-related disasters to seaborne armadas changing the fortunes of their nations. Yet, after long, intense thought, for a reason he himself could not later recall, he announced to his circle of advisors, "I am quite positive we must give the order. I don't like it, but there it is .... I don't see how we can do anything else."[56]

The Endless String of Special Factors

These are just a few instances of *hashgachah* that turned D-Day into the "beginning of the end" of Nazi Germany.

Some others are:

I. The Nazis had scheduled war games for the morning of June 6, which drew more than a half dozen top-ranking German military officers away from the battle area. And what mock invasion were they pretending to play? An Allied invasion in Normandy!

II. The German air force was left with only two fighter planes in the area, where the day before there had been over 125! The German air force commander's response that morning to a call from headquarters suggesting he put his wing on alert was: "Alert! Alert!" he shouted into the phone. "I'm alert! My other pilot is alert! We're all alert! You idiots only left us with two planes!"

✦ ✦ ✦

What can we glean from all this? Don't sleep late in the morning? Don't leave the front to visit your wife on her birthday? Or, perhaps, that there's no such thing as coincidence! And that secular history can be turned into a Torah lesson!

Of course, the greatest lesson is, *"The heart of the king is in the hand of Hashem …"* (*Mishlei* 21:1). For, "Who" told Eisenhower to invade despite the great risk? "Who" manipulated Rommel to leave the front? "Who" saw to it that fifty or so years earlier a baby— who would become Rommel's wife—should come into the world on June 6? "Who" gave Hitler the idea that he should have control over mobilizing those tanks? "Who" made him sleep late, and who made his aide ignore the reports of a possible invasion? "Who" put in the minds of the Nazi commanders to schedule a war game for June 6, leaving a mere two planes in the invasion area? And "Who" caused the other myriad "coincidences"?

On a deeper level, the "king and his ministers" are our own heads and hearts. Shlomo Hamelech's statement does not only concern *hashgachah klalis*, Divine Providence over nations; it also refers to *hashgachah pratis*, Providence governing the details of our individual lives. If we gaze into our own lives, perhaps we may see a little spark of evil that grew and rose to hold great power. We might also see how we overcame it when *Hashem* battled for us, advising the evil within us to let its guard down.

We must teach others and ourselves about all the wonderful *hashgachah* present everywhere we go and in everything we do. Fulfilling this obligation will help us recognize that evil *can* be confronted and defeated; and that it has *no purpose other than to be the victim* of that great and awesome "D-Day" promised us in the future, which we eagerly await.

Smashing Strange Idols

OVERVIEW

It was the last day of the nineteenth century!

City streets across the globe were ablaze with colorful, ornate decorations hung for the celebration. The clamor of whistles, bells, gongs, accordions, rattles and clanging utensils resounded in courtyard and alley, boulevard and lane, as merrymaking citizens took to the streets and danced with joy. Glittering fireworks transformed night into day, adding to the excitement.

A new century was about to begin.[57]

✦ ✦ ✦

The turn of the century was an exciting time for much of the world populace. The ideals of Enlightenment[58] in the previous century filled people with hope. Many believed that civilization had at last progressed to a point where it could look forward to universal brotherhood (emancipation), economic equality (communism), comfort (technology) and peace.

But by the second decade of the twentieth century, those hopes had been obliterated. The deaths of 30 million people—5,000 to 50,000 a day in the "brutal, mud-filled" trenches of "The Great War"—as well as the untold suffering and uprooting of countless tens of millions more, buried the belief that civilization had "turned the corner on barbarity,"[59] toward peace, brotherhood and enlightenment. "When at last it was over," historian Barbara Tuchman writes, "the war had many diverse results and one dominant one transcending all others: disillusion."[60]

As natural idealists, many Jews had also been caught up in these hopes. The nineteenth century saw Jews from every corner of Europe exchanging their religious ideals for secular ones. Eighty percent of Western European Jews assimilated or converted. In Eastern Europe, Poland and Russia, Jews, even those outwardly observant, were experiencing internal decay like never before. Jews fled the shtetls to join anarchist, communist, socialist and bundist movements in the hope of changing their situation in Russia. Instead of Torah, they sought a new "messiah" in the utopian vision of Marxist communism.

✦ ✦ ✦

By the end of the nineteenth century, many Jews began to discover the emptiness of their non-Torah ideals. The Dreyfus Affair[61] was like a bucket of cold water splashed in their faces. And what the Dreyfus Affair was to the late nineteenth century, the Kishinev pogrom was to the early twentieth.[62]

One self-proclaimed Jewish atheist described the profound effect the Kishinev pogrom had on him. "My previous cosmopolitanism, internationalism, and similar ideologies vanished at one blow, like the contents of a barrel with the bottom knocked out."[63]

Rabbi Elchanan Wasserman summarized the situation in his classic essay, *Ikvesa D'Meshicha* ("The Epoch of the Messiah"):

> "Let us now review all the 'idols' which were worshipped in the last hundred years. The 'enlightenment of Berlin' (or better, foolishness) promised a great salvation. As soon as the breeze of Liberalism began to blow, the Jews hastened to stand in the foremost ranks of its exponents. After Liberalism made its exit, they turned to Democracy, Socialism, Communism, and to the other 'isms' that have come down upon our generation in such great profusion. To these idols, they made sacrifices of blood and money—and were betrayed by all of them. Not even one justified the faith that they had pinned on it ..."

✦ ✦ ✦

In this section, we tackle some of the romantic notions worshipped as "strange gods" in modern times and in various events of the twentieth century, which exposed them as fraud.

One is the apparently lofty ideal of liberty; another is the dangers in the worship of money; a third, the notion of our heads of state being imbued with altruistic integrity, and a fourth, another fraudulent ideal, communism. Within each of the incidents described lie small sparks of *hashgachah*, to help us remember Who is really controlling our world.

Of
Statues, Liberty
& Freedom

This is an undated photo of a group of immigrants arriving at Ellis Island in New York. They are waiting in line to begin immigration proceedings. Abut 16 million people came through Ellis Island from 1892 to 1924. (AP Photo)

"Here is not merely a nation,
but a teeming nation of nations."

(WALT WHITMAN)

August 3, 1492. Three painted wooden sailing ships—the Nina, the Pinta and the Santa Maria—bob in the sun-spangled waters off the Spanish port of Palos. Christopher Columbus stands at the helm of the largest ship, the Santa Maria, a bare eighty-two feet long. His anxious sailors, who fear falling off the edge of the earth or being swallowed whole by sea serpents, await their captain's command. At last, Columbus gives the order; each ship's anchor is raised, sails are hoisted and dock ropes released. Masts flapping, the three ships head out to sea to find a new passage to the East. There is no cheering, no flag-waving, no fanfare at all. No one realizes what a historic journey this will be.

No one paid much attention to Columbus, not only because they did not perceive the historic moment as it was happening, but because his tiny fleet was just three among countless vessels of every shape and size trying to exit the port that busy day. Less than twenty-four hours earlier, on August 2, the deadline of the Royal Decree expelling the Jews of Spain on pain of death had arrived.[64] Thus, the Nina, the Pinta and the Santa Maria had to wind their way through a traffic jam of sea vessels over-laden with bedraggled Jewish refugees. Indeed, Columbus wrote in his log about the delay in the harbor caused by the traffic of ships evacuating the Jews.

General history books rarely mention this detail. If they did, the flight of the Jews and the discovery of America would likely be described as little more than two entirely separate events whose appearance side-by-side to each other is at best a peculiarity formed by little more than coincidence. Nevertheless, a bird's-eye view of history reveals a startling pattern, one that transforms Columbus' departure through a port busy with escaping Jews from coincidence into the phenomenon we call "*hashgachah*."

• The Historical Pattern of "Those Who Bless You"

There is a recurring theme in history, which combined with open predictions in the Torah thousands of years old, leads to a conclusion that is no doubt shocking to anyone influenced by a secular approach: Those who bless the Jews will be blessed; and those who curse them will be cursed.

> "And I will bless those who bless you [Avraham], and curse him who curses you; and in you shall all families of the earth be blessed." (*Bereishis* 12:3)

> "And I will make your seed [Yitzchak] multiply as the stars of heaven, and will give to your seed all these countries; and in your seed shall all the nations of the earth be blessed." (*Bereishis* 26:4)

> "And your seed [Yaakov] shall be as the dust of the earth, and you shall spread abroad to the west, and to the east, and to the north, and to the south; and in you and in your seed shall all the families of the earth be blessed." (*Bereishis* 26:14)

Long ago, the Torah said that those who bless the seed of Avraham, Yitzchak and Yaakov would be blessed, while those who cursed them would be cursed. The *Midrash*, also long ago, observed that a) the nations who enslaved the Jews were always at that time foremost among world powers and that b) not long after they banished the Jews from their land, they lost their preeminence.[65]

This pattern began way back in ancient Egypt. When Yaakov first arrived in Egypt, they were friendly to him and his offspring, and Egypt flourished. Thanks to Yosef, the Egyptians prepared for the famine and became extremely powerful and rich. Eventually, they put the Children of Israel in bondage, though. Then Moshe led the people to freedom. Afterward, the Egyptian Empire came undone and mysteriously disappeared from the map of history as a major player in world events.

Centuries later, Nevuchadnezzar exiled the Jews to Babylon before he destroyed the Temple. At first, he let Jews flourish, as the books of Ezekiel and Daniel attest (Daniel himself was a valued advisor and revered figure in Babylon), and Babylon experienced a Golden Age. However, he eventually destroyed the Temple, and within a couple of generations Babylon was conquered by others, the Medes and the Persians.

This pattern was then repeated with Persia: They were benevolent to the Jews in their realm at first, and they in turn flourished. Then they turned on the Jews and experienced downfall.

The Greeks inherited the empire of the Persians. Alexander the Great treated the Jews in his realm favorably. Greece became a world leader. Then things turned ugly, and they persecuted the Jews, leading to the miracle of *Chanukah*. Not long thereafter, Greece was supplanted by the Romans, who at first treated the Jews well and rose to world domination. Then Rome destroyed the Temple, increased persecution to new heights and eventually entered its irreversible slide away from history's center stage.

Jews then found relative sanctuary in the Occident, centered in ancient Babylon—enough to redact the Babylonian Talmud. The same basic pattern repeated itself here, too, where Jews were first shown relative tolerance. Then persecution made Jewish life unbearable, which again coincided with the beginning of that civilization's disappearance as a factor in world events.

Next, the center of Jewish life and scholarship shifted to the Iberian Peninsula (Spain) where the Spanish Moors welcomed Jewish business and intellectual activity. Not coincidentally, Spain then rose to the forefront of world leadership, until it, too, began progressively worse persecution of the Jews, culminating in the infamous Spanish Inquisition and final Expulsion of the Jewish population in 1492. Jews then resettled into various parts of Europe, while Spain, in less than a century, fell ignobly from civilization's leading power to a corrupt, decaying has-been.

Not surprisingly, with Jews scattered throughout the European continent, Europe then came to dominate world civilization. The expulsion from Spain brought Jews to Poland. Benevolent Polish kings and princes granted Jews freedoms that helped make Poland an economic world power, climaxing with the unification of Poland and Lithuania in 1569. Jewish life, institutions of higher education and scholarship flourished. However, it was not to last. During the infamous years of *Tach V'Tat* (1648-49), disgruntled runaway serfs and vagabonds known as Cossacks (from a Turkish word meaning "free men" or "adventurers") revolted against the Polish feudal lords. Led by chief-butcher Bogdan Chmielnicki, they not only defeated the Poles but brutally annihilated hundreds of Jewish communities in their wake, shattering the old orderly and structured lifestyle and eliminating in one swoop the large and prestigious *yeshivos* (Jewish schools) and *kehillos* (communities) that had dominated Jewish communal life. Poland eventually fell off the map of history, politically and literally, when it lost its independence in 1795 and became a puppet state under the regime of the Czars in Russia.

Russia rose in prominence and hosted an equivalent number of Jews as America today, but imploded shortly after an exodus of Jews resulting from the Czar's extremely anti-Semitic policies (see below).

Great Britain had expelled the Jews in the thirteenth century, but Oliver Cromwell reversed the decree in the 1600s. During the ensuing centuries, Britain became the world's leading empire. (England's attitude toward the Jews was mixed in the twentieth century. Although it was England who showed favor to the Jews in 1917 with the Balfour Declaration, mandating a Jewish homeland in Palestine, it reversed its position with the White Papers in 1939 to curry favor with the Arab population when oil was discovered in the Middle East. After the war, Britain not only lost its colonial hold on Palestine, but also most of its other colonies throughout the world that had made it the dominant world power.)

Germany, of course, was Europe's—if not the world's—leading industrial power in the late 1800s. Despite historical anti-Semitism, hundreds of thousands of Jews felt patriotic enough toward the Fatherland to fight and die for it in the bloody trenches of World War I. After World War II, and the Holocaust, Germany lost its claim to industrial, military or moral dominance.

Jews in what is today's Middle East were historically oppressed but generally not to the degree of Jews in Europe. That changed in the twentieth century. Persecution forced countless Jews to leave those lands. Most of today's Middle Eastern states are economically and politically backward, sunk in a quagmire of feudal and/or dictatorship governments whose leaders live in magnificent palaces while the masses live in squalor. Ironically, the Islamic state most tolerant of Jews is Turkey, and they seem to be the least affected, with more freedoms and a wider swathe of their population enjoying the fruits of prosperity.

The pattern of "those who bless you will be blessed" continued into the twentieth century with the emergence of the United States of America. To fully appreciate how, we must analyze some historical details in depth.

• Huddled Masses

Flash back to 1492. Columbus' small ship weaves its way through the Spanish port crowded with ships overflowing with despondent Jewish refugees ....

Now, flash forward about four centuries ....

Another ship—a steam-engined ocean-liner—pitches and

sways on the rough sea. It is packed with about 2,000 passengers (many of whom travel in third class, or "steerage," living for weeks in airless, close quarters in the hold, like cattle[66]). Along the ship's railing, a small boy clutches his father's hand. His eyes follow the gaze of adults peering beyond the ship's railing. The fog, however, is too thick to see anything. "What are they looking for?" he asks.

Suddenly, the man next to them points. Then a young lady points in the same direction. And then everyone begins cheering and clapping. Some fall to their knees and kiss the deck of the ship.

"What is everybody excited about?" asks the boy.

His father picks him up and points. Then he sees it.

It is a tiny, somewhat greenish speck in the sea. As the ship moves onward, it slowly grows bigger and bigger …

And bigger and bigger …

And bigger …

He cranes his neck backward as the ship passes under a colossal statue, standing 305 feet high: the Statue of Liberty.

It is May 5, 1903. As the ocean-liner enters New York Harbor,[67] a small group is conducting a little-advertised ceremony at the foot of the statue. The ceremony centers around the placement of a plaque engraved with the poem entitled "The New Colossus." The poem did not gain true fame for another three decades,[68] but many came to consider it the quintessence of not only what the statue represented—but America herself. The most often quoted stanza reads:

> Give me your tired, your poor,
> Your huddled masses yearning to breathe free,
> The wretched refuse of your teeming shore.
> Send these, the homeless, tempest-tost to me,
> I lift my lamp beside the golden door!

It had been written by a little known poet, Emma Lazarus, who had died in 1887. Lazarus, a *Sephardic* Jew from a wealthy New

York family, was inspired to write her poem after learning of the terrible plight of Jews in Russia in 1881 and 1882.[69]

In those fateful years, the rabid anti-Semite, Czar Alexander III, had passed a series of decrees ("temporary edicts") known as the "May Laws," one of which banished the Jews to the Pale of Settlement, a vast swathe of territory including much of present-day Latvia, Lithuania, Belarus, Poland and the Ukraine.[70] Jews living outside the "Pale," including those in the key cities of Moscow and St. Petersburg, were expelled.

Living conditions in the Pale were horrific: Extreme poverty, hunger and sickness were the norm. Infant mortality was high. Beyond those horrors was the lack of protection from marauders. This was the new Czar's intention. He enabled his government officials to secretly instigate a wave of pogroms across Russia. A pogrom was a *seemingly* sudden attack on the Jews, but one that was usually secretly organized by the local police or government beforehand. These attacks were so vicious and notorious that they created a worldwide outcry, and the Russian word "pogrom" soon became part of the international vocabulary. The ultimate goal of the "May Laws" and the Czar's policy toward the Jews was to cause "one-third of the Jews to emigrate, one-third to accept baptism and one-third to starve."

His strategy succeeded to a great degree. In the decade before he took the throne, an average of 4,000 Jews had emigrated each year from Russia. In the following decade, 1881-1890, that figure rose to more than 20,000 per year. After the "May Laws" of 1881, through 1914, 2.5 million Jews emigrated to the U.S. from Russia. The largest number was recorded between the years 1903 and 1907, when 284 pogroms were perpetrated against Jews.

America became indeed a land of liberty for millions of Jews fleeing Russia and Eastern Europe. It's hard to imagine how they could have survived without her. In this light, it is possible to discern a part of the Divine plan spanning more than four centuries: At the moment that Spain expelled its Jews and opened them to even more horrific persecution in European lands, *hashgachah* was already preparing an important resting place for them: the United States of America. This is a classic example of what the Sages call preparing the antidote before the wound (*Megillah* 13b). Columbus sailing into history to discover the haven that would become known as America at the historic moment Jews were expelled from Spain illustrates this principle poignantly.

This, then, is the first element of *hashgachah* in the story of the Jews and America. However, there is more.

During the time that immigrants flooded her shores, America was transformed from a side-player in world politics to an industrial empire. By the end of the First World War, America was arguably the world leader in industry, military and influence. History books will typically explain that one of the main reasons for this was America's generally liberal policy toward immigrants, which opened the valves to a seemingly endless supply of human energy that fueled America's burgeoning economy and her ascent as an industrial and military world power. However, rarely, if ever, will a history textbook single out the arrival of the Jews for any special significance. After all, Jews are no different than other peoples.

Nevertheless, in the context of the historical pattern of "those who bless the Jews will be blessed; and those who curse them will be cursed," the emergence of America and its benevolent treatment of the Jews adds to the evidence that there is an ancient prophecy at work. Indeed, the United States has been not only a haven for Jews, but arguably the most tolerant country that the Jews have ever lived in. Rabbi Moshe Feinstein, *zt"l,* called upon American Jews to appreciate the compassion and goodwill of the American populace and to thank *Hashem* for His kindness in letting many of His people find refuge under the auspices of this *Medina shel chessed,* "Government of Benevolence" (*Igros Moshe, Choshen Mishpat* II:29). The history of America bears out the prediction in the Torah long, long ago, the promise given by *Hashem* to Avraham, then Yitzchak, then Yaakov: "And I will bless those who bless you, and curse him who curses you; and in you shall all families of the earth be blessed."

Although chances are you won't find this connection in a public education or collegiate textbook, nevertheless, the phenomenon has not been lost on all non-Jewish historians. Professor Huston Smith, author of *The Religions of Man* (pp. 406-7) considered a classic in its field, writes:

> "There is a striking point that runs through Jewish history as a whole. Western Civilization was born in the Middle East, and the Jews were at its crossroads. In the heyday of Rome, the Jews were close to the Empire's center. When power shifted eastward, the Jewish center was in Babylon; when it skipped to Spain, there again were the Jews. When in the Middle Ages the center of civilization moved into Central Europe, the Jews were waiting for it in Germany and Poland. The rise of the United States to the leading world power found Judaism focused there ...."

Historically, the world's fate has been intimately intertwined with the seed of Yaakov. This is not only an undeniable fact, but a prediction made long ago in the Torah, and therefore a vital Torah lesson demonstrating one way *Hashem* has been operating "behind the scenes" in history even unto our day.

• Liberty vs. Freedom

Although America is and has been a haven for Jews, there is a flip side to the coin of liberty that needs to be understood to appreciate the place of America in the ebb and flow of Jewish history.

Freedom has two aspects: freedom "from" and freedom "to." On one hand, freedom means the liberation from something that restrains and confines. Initially, such freedom is exhilarating. But the individual must eventually determine: Where is my freedom leading *to?*

Freedom unto itself does not necessarily lead to goodness and happiness. On the contrary, physical freedom unchanneled leads to spiritual enslavement, since the excess in choices, and the access to every comfort and indulgence, can become overwhelming. When freedom is unfocused, undirected—and completely *unlimited*—it becomes spiritual bondage; actions become inextricably bound to activities of self-induced enslavement. Addiction, illusion, delusion, lies—these are symptoms of freedom unchecked.

How many stories have we heard of well-intentioned people who end up enslaved to their careers, who give up everything to acquire a faster car and larger home, to find in the end that they have neglected their children, their marriage, their very selves?

Freedom for such a person is nothing more than a hollow idol. He has lost touch with the treasure of true freedom, hidden deep inside, which can transform his empty idol into a substantial ideal.

✦ ✦ ✦

When the Jews left *Mitzrayim* (Egypt), they passed through the *Pi Hachiros*, "The Gate [lit., mouth] of Freedom." This place, Rashi tells us (*Shemos* 14:2), was so-named because slaves who managed to reach it through the thick complex of barriers set up by Egyptian authorities could consider themselves free. The Statue of Liberty must have seemed to Jews who had escaped the persecution of Czarist Russia in a similar way: a symbolic gateway where they could actually consider themselves free.

In an even more poignant parallel, *Pi Hachiros* stood opposite the last remaining Egyptian idol, *Baal Tz'fon.* Beneath the temple of *Baal Tz'fon,* the *Midrash* teaches, lay hidden ("*tzafun*" means "hidden") enormous treasures deposited there centuries earlier by Yosef. Superficially, it was nothing more than an idol. At its depths, though, it possessed substance.

The same is true of the ideal named Liberty—in many ways, the last standing ideal of Western civilization. Superficially, like the colossal statue in New York harbor, liberty is a hollow idol. Only when plumbed for its depth does the *idol* become a treasured *ideal* with substance.

✦ ✦ ✦

Liberty and freedom are not necessarily the same thing. Liberty removes bonds and restraints. It provides tangible rights, e.g., the right to vote, the right to due process of the law, the right to hold unpopular views without fear of retribution.

Freedom is more than that. It is not restricted to externals, such as government or powerful individuals. Freedom is *internal* power. Thus, people who live in a land of liberty may sometimes not be free: Their souls may be in prison.

Political revolution may produce liberty, but not necessarily freedom. A person with liberty still needs an *inner* revolution to achieve real freedom. This is why *Chazal* teach: "There is no free person except one who engages in Torah." And this is why *Pesach* (Passover), the "time of our liberty," is followed by *Shavuos*, "the time of our receiving of the Torah."[71]

Pesach represents the escape *from* horrible bondage under Egyptian rule. Release from such devastating oppression is reason enough[72] to celebrate. However, the "freedom from" of the night of *Pesach* is hollow if it is not ultimately connected with the "freedom to" of the receiving of the Torah, which took place on *Har Sinai* forty-nine days later. Liberty is a gift, only when utilized with Torah. Otherwise, it is a hollow idol.

• A Spiritual Wasteland

Although the final chapter of Jewish life in America is yet to be written, the distinction between liberty and freedom, between external freedom and true inner freedom, is a lesson still in progress.

Immigrants flocked to America both for the "carrot" of economic opportunity and to escape the "stick" of ethnic persecution. Most Jews fled to America to escape intolerance and injustice in Europe, and endured the harrowing cross-Atlantic journey feeling the worst was behind them. Even when they discovered that rather than finding "streets paved with gold," as rumor painted it, they would have to work inhumanely long hours at low pay—if lucky enough to find employment—they still believed their lives had improved, and held out hope that the following generations would benefit.

In the material sense, the next generations did; they became part of a booming, world-leading economy. But from the beginning, America was a spiritual disaster for Jews. By 1918, the vast majority of the nearly 300,000 school-aged Jewish children had cast off any residual traces of observance, exclusively attending public schools. According to one survey that year, less than one-fourth of New York City's Jewish youngsters were receiving any Jewish education. Many attended schools associated with the various non- or anti-religious Socialist groups. For those who received some kind of religious instruction, the typical venue was an afternoon Talmud Torah, where boys spent an hour or two after public school learning to read Hebrew and preparing for their bar mitzvahs. There, in an atmosphere of apathy, a poorly paid *melamed* (teacher) to whom English was a second language confronted boys who preferred to be outdoors playing stickball.

Jews had lived in various lands of exile in the past, but had retained their identity far more successfully. What had changed?

In past exiles, the Jewish people had always had Torah institutions and *yeshivos* awaiting them when they arrived in a country. For example:

+ Before Yaakov Avinu and his sons descended to Egypt, he sent Yehudah ahead to set up a *yeshiva* in Goshen.

+ Years before Nevuchadnezzar destroyed the *Beis Hamikdash* (the Holy Temple in Jerusalem), he exiled the nation's leading scholars, who, in turn, set up the first Torah institutions in Babylon.

This was not true in turn-of-the-century America. The first Jews came to America in the Colonial and Revolutionary War times. *Sephardic* in origin, they were few in number and generally not very observant. Large-scale emigration of Jews to the United States began in the 1830s, primarily from Germany. Germany was the birthplace of Reform, and German Jews arriving in the mid-1800s primarily practiced Reform Judaism, deeming assimilation a necessary and desirable step to scale the American social ladder.

Therefore, when Jews arrived from Russia at the turn of the century, they didn't have an infrastructure of Torah awaiting them. Confronted by this spiritual desert, they gradually discarded their traditional way of life. Scrupulous observance of *mitzvos* (Torah commandments), intensive Torah study, holiness and sanctity of personal life all became casualties of the great "Melting Pot" of America.

Most Jews who made it from Europe to New York discovered that America was the "land of opportunity" *only* if you forgot about *Hashem* and religion, especially *Shabbos* and *kashrus* (keeping kosher). If a person told his employer he couldn't work on Saturday, he was told not to bother coming back the next week. If one was lucky enough to have money for food, he couldn't afford to worry whether it was kosher or not.

"G-d has been left on the other side of the ocean," new immigrants were often told.

The millions of European Jews who settled in America between 1880 and 1920 had brought certain commonalities in practice and culture with them, like *davening* (praying) in an Orthodox *shul* (synagogue), speaking Yiddish, buying kosher meat, etc.

Nevertheless, in a short time, often not more than a generation, they had cast off their religious roots and assimilated into the surrounding culture. They had used their newfound liberty to cast off the yoke of Torah. And they did so like never before in Jewish history. The Atlantic crossing thus marked more than a voyage of many miles; it marked a break in the transmission of values, the wisdom and tradition from one generation to another that had once characterized Eastern European Jewish life.

The question is: Why? Why was fate—why was *Hashem*—so seemingly aloof to the plight of the immigrant Jews? Was He abandoning them? Was this a punishment for some communal shortcoming?

• Rabbi Dessler's Principle of Jewish History

Rabbi Eliyahu Dessler, *zt"l*,[73] offers an extremely important lesson about the ebb and flow of Jewish history that may shed light on these questions. He explains that *Hashem* brought our nation out of Egypt with open miracles because, having not yet received the Torah, we were ill-equipped for spiritual growth and had to be saved miraculously. Torah is the means for people to discover and earn *on their own* the spiritual truths beneath the surface of their lives. The Jews in Egypt had not yet been given the wherewithal, the tools, to do it on their own because they did not have the Torah.

In the ensuing centuries after the receiving of the Torah, Rabbi Dessler writes, *Hashem* at times withdrew His Illumination, appearing to have abandoned us. However, the true goal behind this was to give us the opportunity to re-create our faith, our commitment to truth, through our own resources.

This is similar to a father teaching his son to ride a bike. When the father thinks the son is ready, he will let go of the bike. The son may fall and scrape himself, but eventually he will learn that he can ride himself.

✦ ✦ ✦

The slow but definite resurgence of Torah life in America coincides directly with the establishment of Torah educational institutions.[74] It is impossible to do justice to all of the courageous Torah visionaries *Hashem* brought to the shores of America. The efforts of Rabbi Shraga Feivel Mendelowitz, *zt"l*, called the "father of *chinuch* (Torah education)" in America, are legendary.[75] America had no Day School Movement in the 1930s and no more than a dozen Day Schools in the 1940s. Today, there are over 600 Day Schools. After World War II, there was a major resurgence of Torah life when several outstanding *Roshei Yeshiva* and Torah giants settled in America. The social upheaval of the 1960s, capped off with Israel's miraculous victory in 1967, sent ripples through an entire generation of unaffiliated Jews. American youth began to seek a spiritual home for their restless souls. And so was born the *Baal Teshuva* movement.

Perhaps this is the final test to overcome in our nation's 3,000-year-old march toward its destination. When a nation can reestablish Torah in a spiritual wasteland, where nothing was prearranged, and where there are elements and obstacles impeding the way, what greater testimony is there that it is ready for redemption?

The
Crash & the
Great
Depression

The Bread Line sculpture at the Franklin D. Roosevelt Memorial in Washington, D.C. (Shutterstock)

"… On the seventh day of the Festival [of Sukkos]
the judgment of [the nations of] the world is finalized.
Sentences are issued from the residence of the King.
Judgments are aroused and executed that day."

(ZOHAR, VAYIKRA 31b)

"**F**lalands," **my friend told me,** "starts the lowest and goes up the highest."

And he would know. He was already in eighth grade. I was just a seventh-grader. He had learned about the Stock Market Crash of 1929 last year. The history teacher always began the unit with a mock stock market boom and bust. There were a handful of make-believe stocks: Flalands, AT&T, Goldmine Inc. and others. Everyone started with $100 to buy and sell stocks.

"At the beginning of the third day," my eighth-grade friend told me, "everything goes up and then—CRASH; it all becomes worthless. So make sure you sell everything you have right at the beginning of the third day."

I didn't know then about insider information. And, in truth, it wasn't illegal in 1929 anyway. Armed with this information, I planned to become rich.

On day #1, Flalands opened at $10 per share. The teacher explained about buying on margin. We could put down a tenth of our money, and buy ten times as many shares as the actual money we had. I could put all $100 down on Flalands, and get not just 10 shares but 100 shares. Wow, what a deal!

It was so much fun watching my worth go up. By the end of the first day, Flalands was $15 per share. My 100 shares were now worth $1,500. True, I owed $900, the difference between what I had put down and what I owed on margin. But it was still a $500 profit (which in 1929 money could buy me a hot Model-T car with cash to spare[76]).

The next morning I traded in my 100 shares and received $500, minus $50 for commissions and interest (what a rip-off). I then used my $450 to buy 300 shares of Flalands, again putting a tenth down and buying the rest on margin. True, I owed over $4,000 now, but Flalands quickly went up to $20 per share. Even when I paid what I had borrowed, I would be almost $2,000 ahead.

I traded in my shares and kept buying more, on margin again, of course. By day's end, my original $100 was now worth over $50,000! I owed about $30,000, but I was going to trade it all in before the crash in the morning and come away with at least $20,000 profit. I could retire!

Well, the next day came, and I soon realized that all my other seventh-grade friends also had an eighth-grader who had told them what was going to happen. The aisles between desks were crammed with classmates waiting for the signal to charge the front desk where the teacher (i.e., the bank) handled all transactions. However, our teacher was not about to let the kids trample each other in their panic to be first in line, so he banished everyone in the aisles to the back. I, as luck would have it, had a seat in the front row. When the day's trading began, I was one of three people able to sell everything before the crash.

Because of taxes, inflation and other things that I didn't understand, I was left with barely $1,000. But I had the second highest amount in the class. (The kid with the highest had bought AT&T and made his money with dividends, whatever that was.) All but a handful of us were completely wiped out, without even a penny to our name. I remember how badly I felt only having a fraction of the money I had anticipated; imagine how depressed those who had lost everything—and were not only broke, but in debt—felt. No wonder they called it the Depression, I thought.

• Great Lesson, Great Depression

The Crash of '29, which triggered the Great Depression, is one of the most important events of the twentieth century, and contains great lessons in not only economics and history, but Torah as well.

Until "Black Thursday," October 24, 1929—when the market took a huge dive but then recovered—and "Black Tuesday," October 29—when it crashed for good—the 1920s in the U.S. was characterized by its prosperity. Average income grew steadily throughout the decade and production soared. Levels of investment grew to new heights. At year's end in 1925, the market value of all stocks totaled $27 billion. By early October of 1929 that number had grown to $87 billion. The decade was so wildly prosperous, it was like one long spending spree, labeled the "Roaring Twenties."

In 1928, Herbert Hoover said in his acceptance speech for the Republican Party nomination: "We in America today are nearer to the final triumph over poverty than ever before in the history of any land. The poorhouse is vanishing from among us." Just a few days before the crash, Yale University economist Irving Fisher stated confidently: "The nation is marching along a permanently high plateau of prosperity." People believed the market could go nowhere but up.

Of course, what goes up must come down.

Like my classmates cramming the aisles at the beginning of the third day, "panic" describes the frenzy to sell stocks on October 29, 1929. Within a few hours that morning, stock prices fell so low that they wiped out all the gains that had been made in the previous year! Within two weeks, over $30 billion had disappeared from the American economy.

After the crash, the stock market continued falling, until it bottomed out in July 1932. In the United States, at the depth (1932-33) of the Depression, sixteen million were unemployed—about one third of the available labor force. Franklin Delano Roosevelt was elected in November 1932, promising a "New

Deal"—a set of economic, agricultural and relief policies designed to alleviate the effects of the Depression. Although the "New Deal" helped, it is generally agreed that complete economic recovery was not achieved until the early 1940s.

• The Human Toll

The Great Depression was "great" in comparison to any previous economic malady because of its unprecedented length, and the wholesale poverty and tragedy it inflicted on society. Suicide and mental illness skyrocketed; families were torn apart; children dropped out of school and took menial jobs to help support the family; homelessness was rampant. (Around the country, the homeless built settlements of cardboard and tar-paper shacks, called "Hoovervilles" in sarcastic reference to President Hoover.)

There are many stereotypical images of the Depression: long bread lines, hoboes hopping freight trains, former executives selling pencils or apples on street corners, "Okies"—Oklahoma farm families packed into rusty pick-up trucks, their meager possessions roped on behind, off to find migrant farm work in California, as is most vividly portrayed in John Steinbeck's novel *The Grapes of Wrath*.[77]

In the summer of 1932, 25,000 veterans of World War I— who dubbed themselves, "The Bonus Expeditionary Force"— marched on Washington and set up a tent city in front of the White House. Desperate, with hungry families and no jobs (and little prospect of finding one), they were here to demand the bonus Congress had promised veterans in 1924, and scheduled to be paid in 1945. They vowed to stay until they got their money. Although it was a peaceful demonstration, a nervous President Hoover called in the army, which broke it up with cavalry horsemen wielding bayonets, tanks and gas. The veterans were scattered, their jumbled make-shift camp was destroyed and over

100 people were hurt, including two babies who suffocated during a gas attack.

The country was in shambles, economically and psychologically.

⁍ Torah Lessons

There are various Torah lessons one can derive from the Crash that triggered the Great Depression.

First, October 24, 1929, the "Black Thursday" that marked the beginning of the Crash, coincided with *Hoshana Rabba* in *Eretz Yisrael*. The *Zohar* teaches that *Hoshana Rabba* is the day when the economic future of the non-Jewish nations is judged and finalized.[78] How appropriate it is that the day that ushered in the Great Depression was none other than *Hoshana Rabba*.

Second, the "Roaring Twenties" received its name from the effects of material abundance, which led to the idolization of wealth. This age was characterized by the "speakeasy"—the dens of debauchery filled with people roaring drunk with merrymaking, living excessively lavish lifestyles, their morals loosened and all inhibiting influences torn down.

Wealth is a tremendous test. It can cause its owner to become too sure of himself and fall into careless, unrestrained behavior. One must be vigilant and cautious and maintain spiritual integrity, lest he fall into the trap of wealth. Divine judgment over human actions is subtle, but certain.

And a similar idea is seen in the buying of stocks on margin, which almost all historians cite as one of the main causes of the Crash. "Easy-money" lulled people into a false sense of security and wealth. They didn't think about the day of reckoning, until it happened: the day the market crashed. Similarly, when people act immorally and "draw funds," so to speak, from their moral bank account, *Hashem* waits out the situation, hoping people will use their free will to turn their lives around and return to a moral, holy way of living. However, if they don't, there will be a day of reckoning. Debts will be collected. Woe to the person who has not prepared for that day.

America, the world leader, boldly imprints on its coins and paper bills, "In G-d we trust." The Crash of '29 shattered the god of material wealth—a flimsy security to put one's trust in. Greatness is the ability to achieve spiritual gain even in circumstances of want. "All is in heaven except the fear of heaven." When the wheel of fortune turns and wealth is withdrawn, one learns a great deal about oneself, one's people and one's culture, and where one's trust truly lies: in the Almighty G-d, or the not so "all-mighty" god of materialism.

• *Hashgachah* at Work

Despite these and other Torah lessons, the Crash ultimately had a very concrete effect on the Jews, although the effect would not be seen for years. The crash in the U.S., as well as the Great Depression, had a ripple effect on the world economy. Since American businesses could no longer afford to buy raw materials or finished goods from abroad, countries that depended on the U. S. for trade were disastrously impacted, resulting in many bankrupted businesses and unemployed workers.

These happenings would eventually unleash the nightmare of the twentieth century, what came to be called the Holocaust. When the market crashed in America, banks could no longer afford to lend money to Germany. The German economy collapsed once more and many Germans once again found themselves in the street. By 1932, a third of all German workers, some six million people, were out of work and on a breadline. The groundwork was set for the rise of Hitler.

How
Watergate Saved
Jewish Lives

Richard M. Nixon waves a final farewell from the helicopter steps as he leaves the White House for the last time after resigning as President on Friday, Aug. 9, 1974. (AP Photo)

"The Protector of Israel neither sleeps nor slumbers."

(TEHILLIM 121:4)

M ay 31, 2005—the identity of the most famous unidentified person in American history is confirmed. Enfeebled, ninety-one-year-old W. Mark Felt, formerly the number two man in the FBI, is the man who was known as "Deep Throat" in the early 1970s.

"Deep Throat" released the forces that set in motion the Watergate scandal, which ultimately caused the first and only resignation by a president of the United States, Richard M. Nixon.

Watergate, in turn, pushed—albeit unwittingly and somewhat reluctantly—Nixon into the role of savior for millions of Jews during one of the most dangerous times—for Jews and the world—in recent history.

• The Break-In & Beyond

Watergate was the name of the hotel where members of the Democratic Party had rented office space to plan the presidential election of November 1972. And they needed the planning. Their candidate, George McGovern,[79] was well behind incumbent Richard Nixon.

At about two A.M. on June 17, 1972, a security guard noticed that a piece of tape on the door between the basement stairwell and the parking garage was holding the door unlocked.[80] He alerted police, who immediately dispatched three officers. The policemen arrived and surprised the intruders, who surrendered peacefully. The burglars were carrying "sophisticated [bugging] devices capable of picking up and transmitting all talk, including telephone conversations," as well as almost $2,300 in cash. Most strangely, the cash consisted of "$100 bills with the serial numbers in sequence."[81]

At the courthouse the next day, twenty-nine-year-old reporter Bob Woodward, a cub reporter for the *Washington Post*, took notes. (The paper obviously didn't think the story was important enough to send out a more senior reporter.) The defendants already had lawyers representing them, unusual for common burglars, including a very upscale lawyer who claimed he was there just observing. More surprisingly, one of them admitted he had worked for the CIA.

The next day, Woodward—with the help of fellow reporter, Carl Bernstein—discovered that the burglar who had worked for the CIA, James W. McCord Jr., had a contract with the Republican National Committee to provide them security services, i.e., to protect the Republicans from the very bugging devices he was installing in the opposition's headquarters! (Later research revealed that McCord not only had a contract but was the security *director* for the "Committee to Re-elect the President," a fund-raising organization whose goal was to get Nixon re-elected.)

In its early stages, the implication of the break-in was that the Republicans were tapping the offices of the Democrats to stay a step ahead of their campaign strategy. At the time, no one suspected the operation was known—and had been authorized!—by President Nixon. He was comfortably ahead in the polls. Why would he risk authorizing something so unethical; the gain could hardly be worth the potential loss. Speculation at this point, therefore, was that, at most, underlings independent of the President and his staff had done this on their own. Indeed, the White House press secretary told reporters it was nothing more than a third-rate burglary and disavowed any involvement of the White House in it.

However, over the ensuing months, details of the "third-rate burglary" would unfold like a spy novel, transforming it into a scandal.

• Hitting A Wall

By the end of the summer, Woodward and Bernstein had hit a wall. Some of their setbacks were inevitable, but some seemed downright contrived. For instance, during a phone conversation, a librarian at the White House first freely admitted that one of the suspects took out some books, but later the same day, denied the conversation with the reporter ever took place. It was as if someone had gotten to her in between.

Toward the end of September, Woodward and Bernstein discovered that a $25,000 cashier's check earmarked for the Nixon campaign had shown up in the bank account of one of the Watergate burglars. Money donated for a presidential campaign is supposed to be used for advertisements and rallies, not for wiretapping the opposition.

Still, the Watergate story seemed to be fading in significance in the public's eye; with the election approaching, Nixon was still primed for a landslide victory.

Then "Deep Throat" stepped in.

• The Stuff of Novels

Until now, Woodward had communicated with his source by phone. However, "Deep Throat" now became uncharacteristically nervous and warned Woodward not to use the phone; it could be tapped. The reporter should place a flowerpot on his balcony as a signal that he wanted to talk; and if "Deep Throat" wanted to communicate, he would ink in a clock face on Page 20 of Woodward's daily *New York Times*.

To meet, Woodward was to take a taxi in the wee hours of the morning, get out and hop into another taxi heading in the opposite direction, then switch to a third taxi, disembark and finally walk a considerable distance on foot to an empty underground parking garage, where "Deep Throat" would be waiting.

This was the stuff of Hollywood espionage tales.

One thing he made clear right away: He would not *provide* information; he would merely "confirm information that had been obtained elsewhere and … add some perspective." And Woodward could never quote him, even as an anonymous source.

Woodward had reason to believe John Mitchell, the Attorney General of the United States—i.e., the government's top legal adviser—was involved. "Deep Throat" confirmed that Mitchell personally controlled a secret fund used to finance widespread intelligence-gathering operations against the Democrats. Woodward wrote the story and the *Post* published it on September 29.

Mitchell, of course, denied it, but pieces of the puzzle were coming together. Professional burglars, some with links to the Republican Party, get caught wire-tapping Democratic Party headquarters. Twenty-five thousand dollars raised to re-elect Nixon is linked to one of the burglars. The U.S. Attorney General is discovered to have been in charge of a secret fund designed to undermine the opposition. All fingers were beginning to point toward the White House. But could it really be so?

• Deep Throat to the Rescue

Despite the revelations, with a little more than a month until the election, Nixon was still comfortably ahead of McGovern, who had tried unsuccessfully to use the Watergate scandal to win votes. The link between Watergate and Nixon was either not believable or unable to fully condemn the President. That's when "Deep Throat" realized he would have to be more forthright.

In early October, he and Woodward met for almost five hours

in the parking garage. At one point, Woodward argued that he and Bernstein needed something that went beyond the generalities.

As recorded in *All the President's Men,* Woodward and Bernstein's Pulitzer Prize-winning book:

> Deep Throat stopped and turned around. "It was a White House operation—done inside the gates surrounding the White House and the Executive Office Building. Is that enough?"
>
> Woodward grabbed Deep Throat's arm and told him he was still being too general. What did he mean by that; how many people were involved and what did they do?
>
> Deep Throat let out a breath and then told Woodward that the White House had hired more than fifty people to spy on and sabotage the Democrats. Among the tactics they used were: bugging, following people, false press leaks, fake letters,[82] canceling campaign rallies, investigating campaign workers' private lives, planting spies, stealing documents and planting provocateurs in political demonstrations.
>
> Woodward was stunned.
>
> "Fifty people directed by the White House to destroy the opposition, no holds barred?"
>
> Deep Throat nodded.
>
> "The White House was willing to subvert—was that the right word?—the whole electoral process?"
>
> Another nod. Deep Throat looked queasy.
>
> "And hired fifty agents to do it?"
>
> "You can safely say more than fifty," Deep Throat said. Then he turned, walked up the ramp and out. It was nearly 6:00 A.M.[83]

• A Massive Campaign of Political Spying & Sabotage

Shortly after that meeting, the *Post* published a story in its issue of October 10, 1972, less than a month before the election. It described the Watergate break-in as a single example of a "massive campaign of political spying and sabotage conducted on behalf of the Nixon reelection effort."

The Nixon camp immediately issued denials, as well as threats to prosecute the *Washington Post* for false accusations. The nation was still asleep, and on November 7, Nixon was reelected in a landslide victory, garnering over 60% of the popular vote, 520 of the 537 electoral votes and 49 of the 50 states (McGovern carried only Massachusetts and Washington, DC). Nevertheless, the *Washington Post* and others continued publishing stories on Watergate.

◆ ◆ ◆

While all this was happening, Nixon was making history in foreign affairs. In February 1972, Nixon had made an historic visit to Communist China. Even as Watergate was hitting the papers, the nation was reveling in this new relationship with China, a potentially dangerous superpower. This move strategically leveraged the United States' position with the Soviet Union, whose leaders were terrified of the potential new alliance against them, and thus felt a great urgency to improve relations with the United States. This led them to sign the first Strategic Arms Limitation Talks (SALT) treaty, and then the Anti-Ballistic Missile Treaty, which reduced the production of offensive nuclear weapons. Even Nixon's strongest critics had to admit he was pushing the right buttons in foreign affairs. The greatest coup of all for Nixon, however, took place in January 1973 when, with the help of Secretary of State Henry Kissinger,[84] he ended the Vietnam War.

All this should have made him an enormously popular President. However, once Watergate dominated the news, press interviews invariably turned to interrogations about his knowledge of the latest Watergate intrigue.

In January 1973, the original Watergate burglars and their

immediate superiors (Gordon Liddy and E. Howard Hunt) went to trial, and were convicted. However, the convictions not only failed to quell the scandal, but expanded it. The Senate initiated investigations of Nixon's staff, which soon led to the resignations of the President's most powerful aides, Bob Haldeman and John Ehrlichman, on April 30, 1973. That same day, Nixon fired White House counsel John Dean who, sensing that he would become the scapegoat, refused the President's request to compile a report on Watergate to deflect attention from Nixon's involvement.

Dean now became the key witness against Nixon. On June 25, he delivered condemning testimony against many administration officials, including himself, fund-raiser and former Attorney General John Mitchell, and Nixon.

Then, on July 13, the investigators discovered that Nixon had installed a secret tape system that automatically recorded every conversation in the Oval Office. Nixon had planned to use the tapes one day to document his place in history. They certainly would do that, but not in the way he had envisioned.

The investigators subpoenaed the tape recordings. Nixon refused to hand them over. This was virtually admitting guilt. If the President was telling the truth, why wouldn't he release the tapes about the key meetings? The tapes radically transformed the Watergate investigation; it was now clear to the public that the President had something to hide.[85]

• The October War

While America cringed over the newest scandal to their most sacred office of the presidency, on the other side of the world, the Arabs were planning a sneak attack on Israel, scheduled for the holiest day on the Jewish calendar, *Yom Kippur* (October 6). Egyptian President Anwar Sadat had already openly threatened war with Israel in a *Newsweek* interview published April 9, 1973.

Moreover, Israeli intelligence had noted ominous Egyptian troop movements throughout the summer, and had informed the legendary general, Defense Minister Moshe Dayan, who inexplicably decided that attack was not imminent. Just as remarkable, King Hussein of Jordan secretly flew to Tel Aviv to warn Israeli Prime Minister Golda Meir of an impending Syrian attack. (He feared that the Arabs would lose and that the Israelis would annex territory, as they had done in 1967 when Jordan reluctantly joined the war.) Due in great part to a feeling of over-confidence in the Israeli military, all the warnings were ignored.

While Jews across Israel were fasting and *davening* (praying), Syrians[86] in the north and Egyptians in the south attacked, advancing almost unopposed. One story is told of a Syrian general who stopped his tank column because his advance was so swift and easy, he was positive it was an ambush. There was no ambush. The Israelis were caught unprepared.

In the north, Syria was close to cutting off the Jewish communities in the Galilee. In the south, the Israelis' counterattack on October 8 ended in disaster, with the loss of over 400 tanks. (This led Ariel Sharon to come out of retirement and take command of those forces.)

The media soon filled with talk about the imminent destruction of Israel, and a second Holocaust.

The biggest problem was that the Israelis were running out of ammunition. They were brave and well-trained, but could not survive a prolonged Arab assault. It was at this pivotal moment that the events of Watergate came into play.

• Back in Washington

Back in Washington, President Nixon was beginning to crack physically and mentally. It wouldn't be until the following summer that the House Judiciary Committee would recommend beginning the process of impeachment, and not until August 9, 1974, that he would resign. However, as soon as the existence of the tapes became public knowledge, Nixon's physical and mental state deteriorated noticeably. He became paranoid and isolated himself, suspicious of even his closest friends. Amidst this deterioration, the crisis in Israel broke out.

Up until that date, U.S. military support of Israel had remained limited since the Six-Day War. Although the Soviets had supplied Egypt with tens of thousands of military personnel, including more than 100 pilots, as well as MiG fighter jets and sophisticated Surface-to-Air-Missile (SAM) sites after the Six-Day War, Washington kept a short leash on the amount of her supplies to Israel, and what the Israelis could do with them, fearing an escalation of war. As such, by the time the war began, the Soviets were airlifting thousands of tons of weapons to the Arabs, while the U.S. was supplying only limited amounts of ammunition and spare parts to Israel.

While U.S. politicians and militarists hemmed and hawed about helping the Israelis, Nixon surprisingly opened the floodgates and supplied the Israelis with more than they could have imagined. For instance, once it was agreed that the Israelis would be supplied, Nixon's military advisors suggested that the Israelis fly unmarked supply planes to the U.S. to fetch the weapons. Nixon insisted American planes be used. The advisors said that they could only send three planes' worth of supplies. Nixon asked how many supply planes the U.S. had.

"Twenty-five, Mr. President."

"Then fill up all twenty-five and send them all."

"But what about the political fallout?"

"They'll blame us just as much if we send three or twenty-five."[87]

Years later, when portions of Nixon's secret tapes were released to the public, it became obvious that the President was a closet anti-Semite. Racial slurs (albeit not only against Jews) and classic canards—such as how Jews control everything and are inherently duplicitous—rolled off his lips with regularity.

Yet, today history rightfully views Nixon as a friend of Israel. Why did Nixon come to Israel's defense during its time of need? What transformed this closet anti-Semite into such an ally? Obviously, the U.S.-Soviet conflict contributed greatly, since the U.S. always supplied the enemies of whomever the Soviets were supplying. However, the Watergate scandal was at its apex at that time, and Nixon, more than at any other time in his presidency, was concerned about his public image. Despite Israel's victory in 1967, the average American still viewed Israel as the David facing the Arab Goliath. (That view would generally hold true until the Israeli invasion of Lebanon in 1982.) Here was a public relations bonanza lying at his feet. In one swoop, he could gain accolades with a public that identified with the underdog.

Consequently, between October 12 and November 14, 1973, the U.S. shipped 22,325 tons of tanks, artillery, ammunition and supplies to Israel. Resupplied, the Israelis stopped the Syrian advance, counterattacking and driving the invaders back to their original borders, and beyond. They moved within range of Damascus, shelling the outskirts of the Syrian capital.

In the south, Ariel Sharon pulled off one of the most audacious moves in military history, finding the weak link smack in the middle of the vast Egyptian army and crossing the Suez Canal behind them to the Egyptian side. He then held his ground until Israeli reinforcements came. They expanded their hold and trapped the entire Egyptian Third Army in Sinai, threatening them with annihilation. In sudden panic, the Arabs marched on the United Nations, insisting on a cease-fire.

When Israel balked, the Soviets threatened to intervene directly, i.e., use their own airborne divisions to rescue the Egyptian army. The Nixon government responded in turn that the Americans would not tolerate Soviet intervention and, shockingly, ordered the American forces on DEFCON 3, or global alert, which involved even the possibility of using nuclear weapons! Many Americans began to seriously worry about their President's mental stability.

The Soviets yielded to American pressure and World War III was averted. A cease-fire between Israel and Egypt was implemented, and Israel allowed the Egyptian Third Army to return home.

• Lessons

The Yom Kippur War taught many lessons. The Israelis, including their leaders, realized that they had relied too heavily on their military might. They could never again afford to be complacent.

The Arab world, despite their ultimate defeat, could pride themselves that they were not humiliated as they had been in 1967. They also learned about a more powerful weapon than Soviet-made tanks, missiles and planes: oil. And they used that weapon immediately after the war, placing a crippling oil embargo the U.S. and other countries that had supported Israel.

From a Torah perspective, the greatest lesson was that the Savior of Israel "neither sleeps nor slumbers." Jews needed to learn that "not with might and not with armies" is a Jewish army ultimately victorious; that there is no such thing as complete control; we are all, in the final analysis, "clay in the hands of our Maker." Learning this, as they did, on the *Yom HaDin*, the Day of Judgment, sent ripples that are still reverberating through the generations.

The Watergate component of the Yom Kippur War should not be overlooked or downplayed. It pushed Nixon to the edge and caused him to act in a way that far exceeded anyone's wildest expectations, especially given his deeply-rooted dislike for and distrust of Jews. The wisest of men said, "The heart of a king is like streams of water in the hand of *Hashem*. He directs it wherever He wishes." (*Mishlei* 21:1)

So, A) Bob Woodward and "Deep Throat" happened to become acquainted with each other years before Watergate.

B) "Deep Throat" decided to reveal more to Woodward.

C) Nixon decided to bug his own offices.

These three disparate strings came together like estuaries feeding a single river, a river aimed in one direction: to push the most powerful man in the world beyond his limits so he could become a pawn in the true Savior of Israel's design for history.[88]

When the
Berlin Wall
Came Crashing
Down

A man hammers away at the Berlin Wall on November 12, 1989, as the border barrier between East and West Germany was torn down after twenty-eight years, symbolically

"I guess the Experiment failed."

On November 9, 1989, a gloriously sunny day, an unbelievable rumor circulated through the streets of West Berlin. "The East German government is permitting its citizens to leave East Berlin for the first time in 28 years!"

Hearts and minds became choked as people remembered their dear, long-lost relatives who had been incarcerated behind the Wall for so many years. "I'll believe it when I see it," were the comments of many skeptics.

Ermfried Prochnow, a West Berlin taxi driver, didn't doubt the rumor, but believed it would take at least five years, even twenty-five years, before it happened. But as he drove past a corner near the wall, traffic began to slow. Was it possible?

Five minutes later, Prochnow turned into a street jammed with the evidence: Hundreds of revelers were marching toward the wide, ten-foot-high, concrete wall that had separated East and West Berlin for twenty-eight years.

"A traffic jam!" exulted the cabby, who had fled the East just one year before the wall was built. "It's a perfect, beautiful traffic jam!"[89]

The rumor had become a reality. On November 9, 1989, the Berlin Wall began to tumble down—physically, symbolically and politically.

"East Berliners ... forced their way into the no man's land that had been closed to the public for decades. West Berliners clambered over the 10-foot wall and dropped into the arms of those below. East German border police watched, first with detached amusement, and then with undisguised glee. A dozen Western TV crews besieged a group of East German policemen. 'Are you happy?' shouted a reporter. A young guard broke into an enormous grin then turned his back to hide it. Nearby, a young man beat on the wall with a hammer and handed out fragments to the crowd. 'The wall is gone!' the people chanted deliriously. 'The wall is gone.'"[90]

All that day and into the night, great throngs of humanity streamed across the once impenetrable border. Young West Germans stood atop the wall, raising bottle after bottle of champagne to spray on the thousands below who had gathered to watch and to welcome.

"Remember the ninth of November!" shouted a middle-aged man over the roar of the jubilant crowds.[91]

The ninth of November. Truly, a day history was made.

✦ *Fifty-one years earlier, on November 9, 1938, history also had been made. But let's learn more about this wall before we discuss that occurrence and its connection to this November 9.*

• The Iron Curtain

"From Stettin in the Baltic to Trieste in the Adriatic," said Winston Churchill, "an iron curtain has descended across the [European] Continent." It was March 1946, less than a year after the U.S., England and the U.S.S.R. had aligned to defeat Hitler. Churchill's metaphor referred to the Communist Soviet Union's growing ambition to bring much of Europe under its dominion. Using terror tactics, phony conspiracy theories, trumped-up treason charges and other methods, they infiltrated many war-torn, unstable governments like Bulgaria, Rumania, Poland, Hungary and Czechoslovakia, and, with the help of local communists, set up one-party Communist regimes in an ever-widening Soviet sphere of influence.

Those annexed by Soviet Russia were unable to leave their countries, and it was extremely difficult for an outsider to enter any part of the Soviet empire. This situation began to unravel the diplomatic ties between the U.S. and England and the U.S.S.R.. Any warm feelings that had existed between these former Allies, who had waged war together against the Nazi Empire, had grown cold. And the "iron curtain," as Churchill labeled it, formed the boundaries between opponents of a new type of war, a war fought without guns or rockets firing, the "Cold War."

Germany now became a bone of contention. She had been divided by the Allies after her defeat in 1945, each receiving a chunk. The U.S.S.R.'s piece included the capital city, Berlin, which had also been divided by the victors. The Allies were supposed to occupy and govern Germany in a body, but the Soviets weren't cooperating. They annexed their section to become part of the Soviet empire and set up a communist government, thereby dividing the country into an "East German" communist section, with a West German section occupied by the U.S. and other Allies. This caused the western section of the capital city, Berlin, lying deep within the Soviet-controlled eastern part of the country, to become "West Berlin," a tiny island of Western democracy in an ocean of communism.

Suddenly, in June 1948, the Soviets closed all traffic and arteries into West Berlin, violating all agreements between the two sides and threatening more than two million people in West Berlin with starvation. The Western allies were in a quandary. Should they concede West Berlin or resist, risking a third World War just after the second had ended? They chose the middle ground and began a massive airlift of food and materials into besieged West Berlin. Day after day, Allied aircraft flew over Soviet positions with desperately needed supplies. Days turned to weeks, turned to months. Ultimately, 277,804 flights were made, and over two million tons of food and supplies (especially much needed coal for the bitter winter months) were delivered. Finally, on May 12, 1949, the Soviets yielded and lifted the blockade.[92]

The blockade deepened American commitment to West Berlin,

and to all of Europe. Through the Marshall Plan, the U.S. began pumping $12 billion (more than ten times that in today's dollars) into Western Europe to help them rebuild, hoping to contain[93] Communist expansion, which would be more successful in impoverished lands.

The blockade also forced a permanent wedge between the United States and the Soviet Union. These two superpowers would be on the verge of war for the next forty years, stockpiling enough nuclear weapons to destroy the world several times over.[94]

• Anatomy of the Wall

When the blockade was over, the citizens of both East and West sections of Berlin continued to move freely among each other, even after 1952, when the border between East and West Germany was officially closed. More than two million East Germans crossed into the West between 1949 and 1961, almost exclusively through West Berlin.

This was greatly embarrassing to the Communists, as it suggested that people were unhappy under communist rule. It also caused a strain on their pool of human resources. Professionally skilled workers flocked into the West, where they would be recompensed properly for their abilities. (The entire Mathematics Department of the University of Leipzig defected.) Finally, Soviet leader Nikita Khrushchev ordered a barrier placed on the border to prevent defection to the West.

In 1961, a barbed wire fence was raised, and the streets under it torn up to make them impassable to most vehicles. In 1965, a concrete wall replaced the barbed wire. (Additionally, the whole length of the border between East and West Germany was closed with chain-fences, walls, minefields and other installations.) The Wall was over 103 miles long, protected by an inner border as a "no man's land." This hazardous area provided no cover, offering a clear field of fire to the watching guards. It was mined, booby-trapped and paved with raked gravel, making it easy to spot footprints left by escapees, effectively imprisoning the Germans living on the "wrong side."

From 1961 until the Wall came down, about 5,000 people successfully escaped into West Berlin. More than 100 were killed while trying to cross, and another 200 seriously wounded. Among the successful escapes were the more than 50 people who crawled through a 475-foot tunnel dug by West Berliners. One of the last escapes occurred when two men flew fixed wing gliders over the Wall. The most notorious failed attempt took place on August 17, 1962, when Peter Fechter was shot and left to bleed to death in full view of the Western media.

• Backed Against the Wall

Ronald Reagan became President of the U.S. in 1982, and he initiated a change in diplomacy regarding the U.S.S.R.. Whether the Soviet Union was already a disintegrating giant or his tactics were working, by the end of Reagan's second term, serious cracks began to appear in the Soviet air of invincibility.

On June 12, 1987, Reagan visited the Brandenburg Gate in Berlin. This landmark had been the proud symbol of German unity for two centuries, until it became inaccessible after the building of the Wall. He spoke, and ended with a message for the head of state of the U.S.S.R., saying: "General Secretary Gorbachev, if you seek peace, if you seek prosperity for the Soviet Union and Eastern Europe, if you seek liberalization: Come here to this gate! Mr. Gorbachev, open this gate! Mr. Gorbachev, tear down this wall!"

This dramatic rebuke reverberated to the Eastern side of the Wall, setting in motion a rebellious upheaval of the communist regime. By the fall of 1989, there were mass demonstrations against the East German government. In response, long-time East German leader Erich Honecker defiantly predicted that the Wall would remain standing for 100 years. And most Western analysts were quick to agree.

Yet if Honecker's message was so strong, how could November 9, 1989, ever have taken place? It was actually initiated through a mistake. An East German official, Gunter Schabowski, mistakenly announced during his live-broadcast that travel restrictions across Berlin would be lifted *immediately*. In sudden spontaneity, tens of thousands of people converged at the Wall. Unprepared and vastly outnumbered, border guards did not know what to do. Fearing for their own safety, they allowed the masses of people to pass through, with little or no interference.

And, impossible though it seemed, a small chunk of the wall disappeared the following day. And some more disappeared the next day. Slowly, the gap widened. Eventually, police arrived and began bulldozing new crossings and at last the Wall was completely destroyed. Today, pieces of the Wall exist as mere souvenirs on mantelpieces.

• The *Kristallnacht* Connection

November 9—the day the Berlin Wall was demolished—should clearly be the date celebrated as a National German Holiday. However, since it took almost a year of political maneuvering— until October 3, 1990—for East and West Germany to sign agreements reuniting them into a single, democratic Germany, the official date of commemoration is October 3.

Wouldn't the Germans prefer the actual date—November 9, when they physically demolished the wall—as the celebrated date? Possibly. But November 9 is already a memorable date in German history—one the Germans would rather everyone forget.

November 9, 1938, is the date of *Kristallnacht*, the "Night of

Broken Glass," which many mark as the start of the Holocaust. Naturally, Germany would not want a day of celebration to fall on the very date commemorating a black mark on their collective character. Politically, modern Germany maintains a fiercely anti-Nazi stance, and publicly evinces shame for the reprehensible behavior of an earlier generation toward Jews.

• Midah K'neged Midah

Perhaps we may pose a deeper connection here. Twenty-eight years of imprisonment behind a wall under communist rule might be seen as a small piece of the payback *Hashem* is serving the Germans with for the nightmare of *Kristallnacht*, and the forces that night set in motion. One of the earliest and most visible symbols of Nazi oppression of Jews was the ghetto wall, wherein they thrust numerous helpless Jews before starving them and deporting the survivors to death camps. The walls that confined the Jews to an inhuman fate, that separated them from the normal life experienced by non-Jews on the other side, was resurrected symbolically, to a degree, through the Berlin Wall. Communist Russia was a brutal ruler. Instead of the Gestapo, the KGB and other spy organizations could whisk a person away without trial, never to be seen again. Those who weren't killed lived in constant fear. The East Germans, East Berliners and millions in other Eastern countries who often had been willing collaborators in the Holocaust, had to endure these conditions for twenty-eight years.

This does not prove that justice was served, since the Torah teaches us that "The Great Accounting" awaits each individual murderer, an accounting much more painfully profound than any experience this world can offer. Nevertheless, on a collective level (and sometimes on an individual one), there is an obvious lesson here regarding the concept of *midah k'neged midah*: A person is paid back "measure for measure" for his actions. The same follows with a people or peoples. What goes around comes around.

• Epilogue: "I Guess the Experiment Failed"

There's an important epilogue to the story of the downfall of the Berlin Wall. More than just the Berlin Wall fell on November 9, 1989. Within two years' time, the entire Soviet Union would collapse.[95]

The relatively quiet culmination of the Soviet Union was far different from how it had begun some seven decades earlier. On November 7, 1917, revolutionaries stormed the Czar's Palace, killing him as well as his family. Promising "Peace! Land! Bread!," Vladimir Lenin and his followers (the Bolsheviks) unleashed a bloody revolution that would last five years and end the lives of five million people.[96] And when it was over, none of those promises was kept. All land was declared government property. Private farms were confiscated, their owners exiled, imprisoned or simply exterminated. Houses, animals and fine art all became the property of the state. Freedom of the press was eliminated. The secret police (eventually renamed the KGB) ruthlessly squashed all opposition.

Lenin's successor, Josef Stalin, was even more ruthless. More than ten million citizens literally starved to death when he traded their grain for imported factory machinery in an effort to quickly industrialize his backward nation.

Many Jews had joined ranks with Lenin and the original Communists. Leon Trotsky, a *yeshiva* dropout, even rose to second in command behind Lenin (before he was brutally murdered by one of his henchmen). Initially, many of these Jews saw Communism as a way to overthrow the Czars. Eventually, they came to believe in the Communist philosophy itself.[97]

When the Communists came to power, Jews were often at the forefront in oppressing their fellow Jews who clung to their religion. One of the most notorious such group of Jews became known as the Yevsektzia.[98] Sometimes, children brainwashed by the Yevsektzia would even turn in their own parents for practicing Judaism, causing them to be sent to prison or even death. No one could have imagined that not seventy years later their movement would be dead and their ideal exposed as one of the bloodiest and most oppressive in human history.

Rabbi Berel Wein tells the story of his encounter with the daughter of one of the original high-ranking communists. This daughter, now an elderly woman, approached Rabbi Wein after he spoke in Jerusalem.

"Rabbi," she said, "this is the first time in my life that I have ever been to a synagogue. I want to thank you for the wonderful service and your inspiring sermon. I would like to tell you a bit about my background. I arrived from the Soviet Union seven months ago where my family was a model of the communist ideal. We were taught to reject G-d and believe only in the powers of man, science and technology. My father was one of the original members of the Communist Party. Lenin was party member number one; Trotsky was number two; my father was number six. I spoke with him just before he died and his final words to me were: 'I guess we can say the experiment has failed.'"

Rabbi Wein commented on the story: "Imagine. Her father spent his whole life—ninety years!—to build a future on a false dream, on a system destined for failure .... They waste a lifetime trying to create a utopia that cannot exist, all the while ignoring the *eitz hachaim* (tree of life) of the Torah."

The great lesson for Torah Jews is recognizing the bankruptcy of idealism without Torah.[99] Perhaps it was such a realization that fueled the subsequent revitalization of Torah observance among Russian Jewry,[100] and indeed the rest of the Jewish world. If so, the lives of those millions of Jews who poured all their powers into a failed experiment will have gained some meaning.

Smashing
the Idols of
Technology

"In the six-hundredth year of Noah's life ...
all the fountains of the great depth were broken apart,
and the windows of heaven were opened ...."

(BEREISHIS 7:11)

"[This means that] in the year 600 of the sixth
[millennium], the gates of wisdom above and the
wellsprings of wisdom below will be opened, and the world
will prepare to enter the seventh [millennium] just as a
person prepares himself towards sunset for the Sabbath."

(I ZOHAR 117A)

The "year 600 of the sixth [millennium]" corresponds to the year 1840,[101] which uncannily coincides with the Industrial Revolution. This explosion of knowledge continued through the next century and into the current century, growing stronger with the passage of time, like the floodwaters in the time of Noah.

During that same period, belief in G-d weakened as humans advanced in technological expertise and learned to control a great deal of their environment. Mankind grew more arrogant, questioning the need for, or even the existence of, G-d. Perhaps the ultimate expression of this new conceit came from U.S.S.R. cosmonaut Gherman Titov, who purportedly announced to the media when he returned from orbiting the Earth in 1961 that he hadn't seen G-d. (Someone quipped, "Had he stepped out of his spaceship, he would have!")

Technological progress was given to humanity as a gift from *Hashem*. When the "wellsprings of knowledge" burst into the world in the 1800s, we had a choice. Would we eat from the "Tree of Life" or the "Tree of Death"?

Improving the quality of life through technology should not challenge *Hashem*; it should be a laudable endeavor. The Mechanical Age has certainly given us many comforts and allowed us time for worthier occupation. Even moonshot and space shuttles have their place.[102] However, progress without humility—without humanity, without respect for life and the Life-Giver—is a recipe for disaster.

Many times, especially during the twentieth century, we have received loud unmistakable warnings that our arrogance has overstepped itself. Both the *Titanic*, which sank before completing its first voyage, and the *Challenger*, which exploded on take-off, should be seen as wake-up calls.

✦ ✦ ✦

The roots of this hubris are planted deep in the human psyche, which can perhaps be traced to the historical period of the Tower of Babel:

Come, let us build a city, and a tower with its head in the heavens, and we shall make a name for ourselves. (Bereishis 11:4)

The *Midrash* teaches that what the people actually were saying was, "We refuse to accept *Hashem* or His rule. Let us make a name for ourselves."

Rabbi Yonasan Eibeschutz made a remarkable comment on this passage over two centuries ago. He described this "Tower" as a ship designed to fly up into the heavens! This suggests that modern technology is not so modern.

Technology is a two-edged sword. Reaching for the heavens isn't necessarily a bad idea; however, if it's seen as a way to storm the heavens and challenge *Hashem*, it becomes a vehicle of death.

One of the fundamental lessons of the twentieth century is that when humans come to rely upon and believe a little too much in the works of their own hands, *Hashem* orchestrates a major disaster to restore us to proper humility and remind us that technology is only a stick in the hand of *Hashem*. It is He who gives inventors their creative gifts and thoughts, and it is He who, with the barest "effort" (the "breath of His nostrils"), destroys them when humans begin to rely more on the "stick" than the "Stick-Holder."

The
Wrights &
the Lights
of Chanukah

Orville Wright is at the controls of the "Wright Flyer" as his brother Wilbur looks
on during the plane's first flight at Kitty Hawk, North Carolina, December 17, 1903.
Made of wood, wire and cloth by two bicycle mechanics, the plane remained aloft for
12 seconds and traveled a distance of 120 feet. (AP Photo/John T. Daniels)

"And I said, Oh that I had wings like a dove!
For then I would fly away ..."

(TEHILLIM 55:7)

The date: December 17. The place: Kitty Hawk, North Carolina. The time: 10:35 A.M.

A large, box-shaped contraption of wood, metal and fabric, with wooden propellers attached to its front, teeters along a 200-foot-long wooden launching track. Engine roaring, the rickety machine lurches forward. As it chugs down the track, onlookers hold their collective breath. This is what history feels like.

The flimsy flyer picks up speed. It rises ... one inch ... two inches ... six inches ... then—PLOP! Twisting awkwardly, it belly flops headfirst into a muddy puddle.

The year? 2003!

This is the reenactment of the famous day in 1903, 100 years ago, when the Wright brothers made their historic flight, ushering in the Age of Aviation. In attendance, witnessing the spectacle, are not the seven men (including the two Wright brothers) who were present in 1903, but 35,000 spectators. The wreck lying in the puddle is not the Wright brothers' "Flyer" (as they called it), but a $1.2 million replica.

Nevertheless, the lesson is timeless: Even 100 years of science and experience do not guarantee success, or achieve Technological Man's ever-fleeting goal of absolute control. A mysterious factor, independent of human will, that can neither be foreseen nor calculated—"timing" or "luck" some would call it—is invariably an intimate companion of progress.

• Dreams of Flight

The Wright brothers' achievement did not originate in a vacuum. They were riding the crest of a wave of progress known as the Industrial Revolution. Humanity was undergoing a radical change. Until now, manufacturing relied on the muscle power of animals or humans, or the power of water or wind. Beginning in the 1700s, and continuing into the 1800s, breakthroughs in science, capped by the inventions of innumerable machines, changed not only the way humans made things, but also how they lived.

Nothing better symbolizes the advances of the Industrial Revolution than human flight. The dream of flight had occupied human imagination for thousands of years. *(See below, pp. 145–148., "Flight Facts.")* The Greeks told the tragedy of Icarus who attempted flight with wings of wax, which melted in the sun, plunging him to his death. Their mythology concocted Pegasus, a winged horse, upon which the son of the king rode into battle. Alexander the Great was said to have harnessed mythical winged animals, Griffins, to fly around his realm.[103]

The Wright brothers, neither of whom finished high school,[104] spent eight years pursuing a dream that the greatest minds of the times were chasing, too. The academic Samuel P. Langley, director of the prestigious Smithsonian Institute, had received a $50,000 grant to design the first motor-powered flying machine of the day. When the Wrights contacted Langley, he was not impressed, considering the brothers, who made their living selling and repairing bicycles, little more than "hobbyists."

• The Dream Comes True

Thursday, December 17, 1903, dawned like any other day in the history of civilization. On North Carolina's Outer Banks, it was cold and windy, with the thermometer hovering around the freezing mark and a stiff 25 mph wind blowing out of the north.

Wilbur stood in position by the right wing tip. Orville pulled the release. The machine began chugging down the track, slow enough for Wilbur to jog alongside for the first forty feet, until it began to rise. Then Wilbur let go and the flyer leaped ten feet into the air. John Daniels, whom they had hired to photograph the event, squeezed the shutter bulb and captured a black-and-white photograph that would be reproduced millions of times and remain forever engraved on the pages of human accomplishment.

Although Orville's first flight was wobbly (the nose bounced up and down) and brief (lasting only twelve seconds, and landing only 120 feet from where he'd started), he became the first person in history to achieve controlled, powered flight in a machine that was heavier than air. Those few 120 feet were truly a giant leap for humankind, catapulting it into a new era.[105] As one journalist eloquently put it:

> "... As Wilbur Wright watched his brother guide their flying machine into the air, the past and the future separated and the world started shrinking. Left behind were weeks-long trips across the U.S. and months-long crossings of the Atlantic Ocean. Ahead lay transcontinental trips of less than a day, and eventually even the oceans would be crossed in a few hours. And then, one summer day a mere 66 years later, men would fly to the moon and walk around on it."[106]

Remarkably, the Wrights' achievement remained relatively unknown to the world for several *years* afterward. In 1908, they finally received international recognition when Wilbur flew their machine before dignitaries in Europe (Orville demonstrated it a month later in the U.S., before the army). In 1909, when Wilbur flew a plane around the Statue of Liberty, the brothers gained celebrity status.[107]

• The *Chanukah* Connection

Since manned flight might be called the archetype of technological achievement, it is fitting that this breakthrough occurred during *Chanukah*. (December 17, 1903 was the 28th day of Kislev 5664, the fourth day of *Chanukah*[108]) The miracles of *Chanukah*, i.e., the military victory over the Greeks and the oil that burned eight days, are reminders that what appears to be the result of human action is nothing more than *yad Hashem*, the "hand of G-d." *Hashem*, not human beings, controls nature and events—even ones seemingly orchestrated by human power and know-how.

Chanukah celebrates the victory of a small band of Jewish fighters over the Greek superpower of its day. The weak vanquishing the powerful reminds us that the victory of one army over another is not about military might and technology. (The Greeks possessed a super-weapon, the elephant.) Victory and defeat are determined by a deeper reality, *Hashem's* will.

Similarly, the ability of oil to burn is considered a "law of nature." But when oil burns on and on for eight days, though that same "law of nature" dictates that it evaporate after several hours, we are reminded that nature's laws are an expression of *Hashem's* will. Nature is simply the will of *Hashem* repeated in a predictable way. If *Hashem's* will is for the unpredictable—the "miraculous"— to happen, then oil for one day will last for eight.

This is conveyed in a Talmudic story about Rabbi Chanina ben Dosa.

One evening, Rabbi Chanina's daughter said, "We have no oil to light candles."

"Do we have vinegar?" he asked.

"Yes."

"So let He who tells oil to burn now tell vinegar to burn."

She lit the vinegar and it burned.

Why does oil burn and not vinegar? Is it really the "nature" of oil to burn and the "nature" of vinegar not to burn? From Rabbi Chanina's perspective, oil burns not because of any "law of nature" but because *Hashem* determines that it do so, each and every time a person ignites it. The physical world is only the outer garb of an inner, spiritual essence—the "will of *Hashem*."

Even technological achievement, the epitome of human ingenuity and control, demonstrates this. After all, who puts the thoughts in a person's mind to invent a new machine? Indeed, the Wright brothers didn't even have a high school education, yet they—and not the scientists and Ph.Ds—discovered how to fly!

Further, we so often see that invention is the product of "luck" and "chance." Wilbur Wright, for example, discovered a key principle of aerodynamics, "wing warping," while absent-mindedly fiddling with an empty, rectangular, cardboard box in his shop while attending a customer. *(See below, "Flight Facts.")*

And how often has it happened that just when we think we have finally achieved full technological control, some disaster results.

Hashem is not disproved by Science. Science is another name for the gift of mind and spirit that *Hashem* grants His creations to help them create a better life through their own efforts.

Nature is a puppet attached to the strings of the Master. It is a mask hiding the Face of *Hashem*. On *Chanukah*, we try to peel back the mask and see that the miraculous is present, prescient, embedded, imminent and revealed.

And if we can see beyond the often-blinding earthly light, we will be privy to a vastly more beautiful light, the Divine light, aglow in the *menorah*'s flickering, eternal flame.

• Flight Facts

+ The Chinese were the first to discover the kite, some time around 400 BCE.

+ In the 1400s, Leonardo da Vinci wrote: "A bird is an instrument working according to a mathematical law. It lies within the power of man to make this instrument with all its motions." He sketched over 100 drawings illustrating his theories of flight.

The modern day helicopter is based on his Ornithopter, a flying machine he designed (but never built) in 1485.

+ In 1783, Joseph and Jacques Montgolfier invented the first hot air balloon. Their first passengers were a sheep, rooster and duck. Their balloon climbed to a height of 6,000 feet and traveled more than a mile. The first flight by humans in their balloon took place on November 21, 1783.

+ In the early 1800s George Cayley spent fifty years designing and tweaking gliders. Otto Lilienthal was the first to design a glider for a person to fly in. In 1896, after more than 2,500 flights, he was killed when one of his gliders crashed to the ground.

+ Around the same time, Samuel P. Langley designed the first plane with an engine. However, his steam-powered engine was too heavy and too weak to sustain flight with a human.

+ Wilbur Wright, age 29, read Otto Lilienthal's book on aerodynamics after hearing of his death. By 1899, Wilbur, a voracious reader, had studied all the available research on the subject.

+ Through a stroke of "luck" that so often accompanies great things, Wilbur discovered an important principle of flight months before arriving in Kitty Hawk for the first time. Fiddling with a foot-long rectangular, cardboard box, while tending a customer in his bicycle shop, it suddenly struck him that the wings of his box-winged glider needed to be able to twist just as the little cardboard box he was holding. When one side twisted up and in, the other side needed to twist down and out. This concept, called "wing warping," became a cornerstone of the Wright brothers' achievement, and, indeed, of the Age of Aviation.

+ The Wrights' "Flyer" used a gasoline-powered engine that weighed 179 pounds and delivered 12 horsepower; each propeller was 8½ feet in diameter, made of wood glued together, shaped with a hatchet; its wingspan was 40 feet, 4 inches; the length from nose to tail was 21 feet; its unmanned weight was 605 pounds. In contrast, a Boeing 747 is 230 feet long, has a wingspan of 211 feet, weighs 870,000 pounds, holds 524 passengers, can reach speeds of 600 mph and fly for a distance as much as 8,400 miles and as high as 45,000 feet.

+ There are several claims of earlier powered flights made by others. However, the Wright brothers were the first to patent a three-axis system of control: roll, pitch and yaw. These principles are still in use in almost all modern aircraft.

+ Wilbur Wright's earliest recollection of his interest in flight: "Late in the autumn of 1878, our father came into the house one evening with some object partly concealed in his hands, and before we could see what it was, he tossed it into the air. Instead of falling to the floor, as we expected, it flew across the room till it struck the ceiling, where it fluttered awhile, and finally sank to the floor … It was a light frame of cork and bamboo, covered with paper, which formed two screws, driven in opposite directions by rubber bands under torsion. A toy so delicate lasted only a short time in the hands of small boys, but its memory was abiding." (From the letters of Wilbur Wright)

+ Reflecting on his accomplishment a decade later, Wilbur said: "After these years of experience I look with amazement upon our audacity in attempting flights with a new and untried machine under such circumstances. Yet faith in our calculations and the design of the first machine, which were based upon our tables of air pressures secured by months of careful laboratory work, and confidence in our system of control—which we developed by charting three years of actual experiences in balancing gliders in the air, had convinced us that the machine was capable of lifting and maintaining itself in the air, and that, with a little practice, could be safely flown."

+ Although the most famous flight of December 17, 1903, was the first one that lasted twelve seconds and traveled 120 feet, the longest flight made that day was by Wilbur around noontime, lasting fifty-nine seconds and traveling a distance of 852 feet.

+ Wilbur Wright was born on April 16, 1867, and died on May 30, 1912, at the age of 45. His father said of him: "This morning at 3:15, Wilbur passed away, aged 45 years, 1 month, and 14 days. A short life, full of consequences. An unfailing intellect, imperturbable temper, great self-reliance and as great modesty, seeing the right clearly, pursuing it steadily, he lived and died."

+ Orville Wright was born on August 19, 1871, and died January 30, 1948 at the age of 77. He served on the National Advisory Committee for Aeronautics (NACA) for 28 years. NASA (National Aeronautics and Space Agency) was created from the National Advisory Committee for Aeronautics in 1958.

+ Michael Foale, a British-born American astronaut serving on the International Space Station, where he was on a 200-day stay with a Russian cosmonaut, Alexander Kaleri, was asked by CNN about his impressions of the Wright brothers' achievement on its 100th anniversary: "I think it's incredible, when you think what's happened in a hundred years," he responded. "It's astounding that maybe half a million people are in the air at any one time above our planet Earth—and that we, Alexander and myself, are two people living above the atmosphere, and moving around the Earth once every one and half hours. When you think that it goes back to a 12-second flight of 120 feet by Wilbur and Orville Wright in 1903, it is incredible."

A
Titanic
Lesson

The liner *Titanic* leaves Southampton, England, on her maiden voyage Wednesday, April 10, 1912. (AP Photo)

Scores of ministers preached that the Titanic
was a heaven-sent lesson to awaken people
from their complacency, to punish them for their
top-heavy faith in material progress.
If it was a lesson, it worked—people have never been
so sure of themselves since ....

(WALTER LORD, *A Night To Remember*)

In 1985, deep-sea explorer Robert Ballard announced a startling discovery: He had discovered the wreck of the *Titanic* at the bottom of the Atlantic.

Lowering his specially made deep-sea diving submarine more than two miles under the sea, he filmed and photographed the ship as she lay in two pieces strewn across the ocean floor. The discovery made Ballard famous and created a buzz about the *Titanic* that has never died down. In the years after Ballard's discovery, others undertook the great expense and risk of photographing the *Titanic*. And still the public craved more. Finally, in 1997, film director James Cameron made a movie centered on the famed ship and its ill-fated maiden voyage.

Fascination about the *Titanic* goes beyond mere Hollywood hype. Indeed, long before Ballard and Cameron, from the moment the world first heard the news of the *Titanic's* sinking, the need to know what happened that fateful night reached such proportions that it cannot be easily explained. This seems to suggest that, on the deepest level, the sinking of the *Titanic* bears a message larger than the demise of one ship. Hidden in the sinking of the *Titanic* is a message that both terrifies and inspires, a message as relevant for people living at the time of her demise as well as a century later.

• G-d Himself Could Not Sink This Ship

The *Titanic* sailed from England on April 10, 1912. It was her maiden voyage. Her destination: New York. Newspapers and other tabloids had already dubbed her "unsinkable." A passenger asked one of the deckhands carrying her luggage onto the ship, "Is this ship really unsinkable?"

"Yes, Lady," he answered. "G-d Himself could not sink this ship."[109]

There was good reason to think so. The *Titanic* was as long as four city blocks and as high as an eleven-story building. She was so much larger than other ships of her day that new docks had to be built on both sides of the Atlantic to service her. Just one of her funnels was large enough to drive two trains through—and she had four funnels. A single anchor weighed over fifteen tons and needed twenty horses to pull it. She carried enough food to feed a small town for several months.

Beyond sheer size, she was designed for safety by an intricate system of sealing off areas, which prevented water in one section from spilling over into another. And she was engineered with the ability to stay afloat even if four of the largest interior sections became flooded. Of course, no one expected to utilize these precautions, since the *Titanic's* captain was a man with thirty-eight years' experience—thirty-eight years, and an immaculate safety record.

The *Titanic* received worldwide attention because her maiden voyage carried an impressive passenger list. Astor, Guggenheim, Strauss—even today, these names are associated with wealth and aristocracy. In the world before movie, radio, television and sports stars, the public depended on socially prominent people to enrich their drab lives.

April 14, only four days out at sea, disaster—in the form of an iceberg—struck. It was a crystal-clear night, and the mammoth ship was traveling swiftly at full steam, [despite numerous iceberg warnings,] when lookouts spotted an iceberg dead in her path. Some experts claim that if the ship had not swerved sideways, but rather had taken the iceberg head on, she would ultimately not have sunk. But as "luck" would have it, the *Titanic* did swerve, and the iceberg sliced a hole large enough to sink her within a mere three hours.[110]

Her overconfident travelers were slow to react to the severity of the collision. Passengers on deck played with chunks of ice that had fallen from the passing iceberg. Gentlemen in first class paused briefly at the sudden jar, but then continued their smoking, small talk and card games. Those asleep in their warm berths never woke up, or fell back to sleep.

Eventually, however, the word spread. The bow (front) had begun to dip ever so slightly … and then ever so slightly more. Flares were fired. (They were spotted by a ship ten miles away, but it never responded.) Slowly, it dawned on everyone that this was no mere drill (although the ship's band came on deck to play upbeat music while the lifeboats were lowered into the sea).

As the bow sank beneath the water, the stern (rear) rose higher … and higher … until the *Titanic's* monstrous propellers emerged from the sea and glistened in the sky. She rose higher and higher … and then her 50,000 tons of metal snapped in half. The front of the ship sank under the waves, while the remaining portion righted itself, standing perpendicular in the air. It stayed that way for a few breathtaking moments … before sliding into the sea.

Tragically, the *Titanic* was equipped with only enough lifeboats for half her passenger load,[111] and even then, most of the boats were only partially filled. After the ship disappeared, hundreds of people thrashed about on the water, many wearing life-vests. But with the water temperature at 28 degrees, most of them froze. Only a few were still alive when a rescue ship arrived, less than two hours later.

• No Coincidences

The Torah teaches that there is no thing as a coincidence. General events—especially the larger sweeping ones—have messages for us to discern because *Hashem* orchestrates them. *Hashgachah pratis*—literally, "overseeing the particulars" or Divine Providence—is often seen in the simple twists of fate at the core of historical events, large or small, that invariably demonstrate that the world has a Master and that we humans are pretty puny in its wake.

Consider the *hashgachah pratis* associated with the *Titanic's* sinking:

1. Had it not been a moonless night, the iceberg would have been spotted soon enough for the ship to slow down in time to swerve without touching it.

2. Had the sea not been uncommonly calm, the froth of waves lapping the iceberg would have alerted the lookouts to the iceberg's presence in time to avoid it.

3. Had they spotted the iceberg a few seconds later,[112] there would have been a head-on collision, and the *Titanic* probably would not have sunk.

4. Had another ship ten miles away not turned off its radio equipment barely ten minutes before the fatal collision, it would have heard the distress call in time to rescue passengers.

5. Had the rescue ship arrived one hour earlier … Had the water been a few degrees warmer, and so on … disaster could have been averted.

At the same time, the Divine precision of *hashgachah pratis* was conspiring to save a remnant of the victims. If the iceberg had inflicted a larger wound … Had there been no rescue ship in the vicinity … Had the lifeboats encountered stormy seas, etc.—none of the passengers would have been saved, and the world would have never known what had happened. Furthermore, had it not been the famed *Titanic*, had it not been her maiden voyage, had she not been dubbed unsinkable, had she not been transporting such prominent people—it would never have made the headlines, not in its own day nor across the decades to intrigue people today.

Yet, all those elements of *hashgachah* did occur precisely in that way because there is a greater message in the sinking of the *Titanic*, a message as relevant for the people at the beginning of the twentieth century as for those at the beginning of the twenty-first.

• The End of an Era

The greater message in the tragedy of the *Titanic* was not lost on the people of its time. Walter Lord's account of the event in *A Night To Remember* concludes:

> Overriding everything else, the *Titanic* also marked the end of a general feeling of confidence. Until then, men felt they had found the answer to a steady, orderly civilized life. For 100 years, the Western world had been at peace. For 100 years, technology had steadily improved. For 100 years, the benefits of peace and industry seemed to be filtering satisfactorily through society ....
>
> The *Titanic* woke them up .... Here was the "unsinkable ship"—perhaps man's greatest engineering achievement—going down the first time it was sailed.
>
> But it went beyond that. If this supreme achievement was so terribly fragile, what about everything else? If wealth meant so little on this cold April night, did it mean so much the rest of the year? Scores of ministers preached that the *Titanic* was a heaven-sent lesson to awaken people from their complacency, to punish them for their top-heavy faith in material progress. If it was a lesson, it worked—people have never been so sure of themselves since ....

A Titanic Lesson

The *Titanic* has been called a cultural metaphor because she so perfectly illustrated the era into which she was born.[113] And that metaphor still resonates today. Doesn't much of modern society's faith still rest on technological, medical and scientific progress? Do we not place inordinate trust in the captains of science and industry to protect us as we plunge into the darkness of worldwide armament? And aren't we equally prone to the pitfalls of wealth, its false sense of security and its ever-encroaching complacency?

The *Titanic* metaphor resonates on many levels, most importantly, because it jerks us out of our provincial view of reality, making us gasp in awe at our sudden recognition of the hugeness of *Hashem's* world and His personal Presence in it. It is like walking aimlessly along a path, when suddenly, unexpectedly, you come to a cliff—and see the Grand Canyon in all its gaping majesty. You feel so small. But in that very smallness, a vista opens up. You see the hand of Providence, and can do nothing but stand back and gape.

• A Parting of the Waters

Interestingly, the *Titanic* set sail on April 10, 1912, which fell out on *isru chag*, the day after *Pesach* (in the Diaspora).

April 15, 1912, the day the *Titanic* sank (it was 2:20 A.M., April 15), was exactly one week after *acharon shel Pesach*, the last day of *Pesach*, a day that commemorates the drowning of the Egyptians in the waters of the Red Sea. The parallel is striking.

Just as the *Titanic* represented the technological might, vast wealth and cultural attainments of the Western world in her day, so, too, was Egypt the pinnacle of might, wealth and culture in its day—yet both were destroyed by water[114] in a fleeting moment. Could there be a more resounding demonstration of the Almighty's incomparable power and control?

• In *Hashem's* Hands

Hashgachah does not mean that events are engineered to come out exactly as we want them to. The passengers on the *Titanic* who drowned included courageous parents and little children. The victims in wars may be innocent civilians and idealistic soldiers. A holocaust takes the righteous along with the less-than-righteous, etc.

Hashgachah opens our eyes to the indisputable evidence of the hand of Providence. In the moment that we recognize it, we become aware of the Presence of the Divine. Once in that Presence, we can gain the perspective to understand that whatever is happening—war, famine, our personal pain, etc.—is in *Hashem's* hands.

Like so many other larger-than-life events in general history, the fate of the *Titanic* stands as another reminder that, in the final analysis, even the most powerful humans are not in control. The world is controlled by its Master, Who manipulates events and Who brings about the phenomenon called *hashgachah*. The *Titanic* may be a ghost ship lying in the depths of the ocean, but her lesson is still here. Her lesson—a message as timely as it is timeless—still haunts the modern conscience.

• *Titanic* Tidbits

✦ In 1898, an obscure author named Morgan Robertson wrote a book called *Futility*, about a fictional ocean liner named the *Titan* because it was the largest ship ever built and was deemed unsinkable. It set sail across the North Atlantic in the month of April, with many rich and famous passengers aboard. Robertson's *Titan* struck an iceberg and sank. Hundreds of passengers lost their lives because there were not enough lifeboats. Morgan Robertson wrote this book a full fourteen years before the *Titanic* sank!

+ The *Olympic*, the *Titanic's* almost-as-huge sister ship, collided with a navy ship on September 20, 1911, opening a forty-foot gash that nearly sank it. The accident raised concerns over whether the new superliners might be too large to navigate properly.

+ Before even leaving the harbor, the *Titanic* came within four feet of colliding with the *New York*, another passenger ship. Only last-second intervention by tugboats prevented the mishap. (Of course, one could speculate that the collision could have delayed *Titanic's* departure, and thereby averted its fate altogether.)

+ The *Titanic* received its first warning of ice ahead on April 12. More warnings were received on April 14 at 9 A.M., 11:40 A.M. and 1:42 P.M.. Captain Smith reacted by altering course to the south, but did not slow down. At 7:30 P.M., the steamer *Californian* reported ice fifty miles ahead. That message was delivered to the bridge, *but not passed to Captain Smith.* At 9:30 that evening, another warning about large icebergs was transmitted, but was put aside because of the backlog of passengers' messages. At 10:55 P.M., less than an hour before *Titanic* would strike the iceberg, the *Californian* warned the *Titanic* again, but the overworked wireless operator curtly beeped back, "SHUT UP!"

+ It took over $100 million in today's money, more than 15,000 workers working ten hours a day, five and a half days a week, with few breaks and no paid holidays, and more than three years to build and fit the *Titanic*. It took two hours and forty minutes for it to sink once it struck the iceberg.

+ The *Titanic* carried 5,892 tons of coal (or about ¼ of its total weight) and used about 600 tons a day when cruising at full speed (21-22 knots).

+ The *Titanic* left port with about 75,000 pounds of meat,

11,000 pounds of fish, 7,500 pounds of bacon and ham, 40,000 fresh eggs, 2,200 pounds of coffee, 800 pounds of tea, 10,000 pounds of sugar, 36,000 oranges, 16,000 lemons, 1,500 gallons of milk, 6,000 pounds of fresh butter, almost 3 tons of tomatoes, 2,250 pounds of green peas, 3,500 pounds of onions and 40 tons of potatoes.

✦ Kosher meals were available on the *Titanic*; the crew included a chef, known as the "Hebrew chef," to prepare them.

✦ Isidore Strauss and his brother Nathan—both among the wealthiest Jews of their time—visited the Holy Land in 1912.[115] At the end of their trip, Nathan decided to stay on, donating a great amount of money and having a new city called by his name: Netanya. Isidore, who had made much of his fortune from his "Macy's" department store in New York, departed with his wife, Ida, for America. They made their way to Europe and boarded the ill-fated *Titanic*, going down with the ship five days later.

✦ Isidore and Ida Strauss had been married for forty-one years at the time of the disaster. They raised six children together. During the sinking, *Titanic's* officers pleaded with the sixty-three-year-old Ida to board a lifeboat and escape the disaster, but she repeatedly refused to leave her husband. Instead, she placed her maid in a lifeboat, taking her fur coat off and handing it to the maid, saying, "I won't need this anymore." At one point, she was convinced to enter one of the last two lifeboats, but jumped out to rejoin her husband. They were last seen standing bravely together on deck.

The Challenge
of the
Challenger

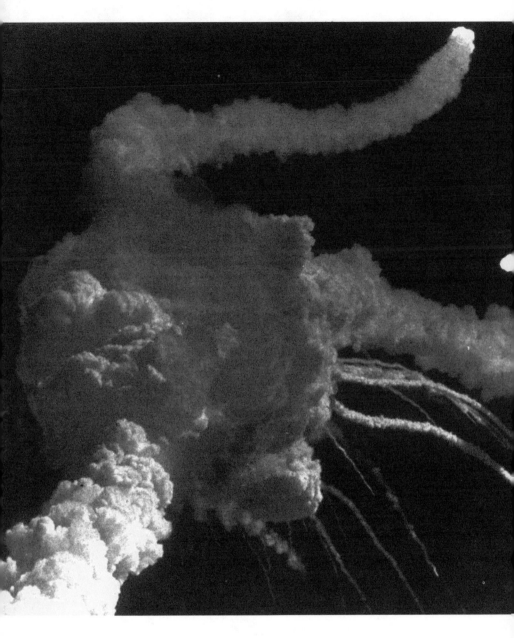

The space shuttle *Challenger* explodes 73 seconds after takeoff on January 28,
1986, at Kennedy Space Center, Florida. The seven crew members perished in the
explosion. One of the shuttle's booster rockets, whose faulty O-rings were blamed
for the disaster, shoots off to the right. (AP Photo/Steve Helber)

And it came to pass, on the third day
in the morning, that there was thunder and lightning,
and a thick cloud upon the mount, and the sound
of a shofar exceedingly loud; so that all the people
who were in the camp trembled ....

(*SHEMOS* 19:16)

January 28, 1986. A slow, deep rumble ... followed by a steady rushing noise. And then—a flash of light ... followed almost immediately by a thunderous blast, increasing in intensity to a deafening pitch. The earth shakes violently. Onlookers, even miles away, shudder, staring transfixed at the blaze of smoke and fire.

Thrusting upwards on a pillar of flames, the cumbersome Space Shuttle *Challenger* rises slowly, finally edging past the launch tower, then surges toward the heavens on a billowing, thick plume of solid white smoke.

"Wow, how pretty," cries an excited little girl.

The twenty-fifth shuttle mission was to be unlike any other. For the first time in history, a civilian would travel into space. Christa McAuliffe, a high school teacher from New Hampshire, had been selected from among over 11,000 applicants nationwide. McAuliffe was to teach millions of American schoolchildren from up in space. She would participate in various scientific experiments, and after the flight, serve as a spokesperson for NASA about scientific careers. Christa McAuliffe was also an extremely personable woman whom everyone liked.

Across the country, millions of schoolchildren were tuned in to watch the launch, including the 550 students at Thomas Johnson Middle School where McAuliffe had taught from 1971 to 1978. By 11:20 A.M. all school activities had stopped. Students were gathered around television sets in classrooms or in the school's large media center. Their excitement was palpable as they watched the *Challenger* climb.

Seventy-three seconds into the flight, two orange balls of fire shot out from either side of the shuttle's white trail of engine smoke. Suddenly, with a deafening crack, the entire craft exploded into an enormous fireball, obscuring the ship completely. Slowly, smoking pieces of debris trailed earthward in wide arcs, like remnants of Fourth of July skyrockets.

Something had gone terribly wrong.[116] As the "recorded-live" catastrophe hit the television screens all over the U.S., observers stood rigid with shock, unable to fully comprehend the enormity of what they had seen. It took a few seconds for the reality of the horror to sink in.

Rescue helicopters and Coast Guard vessels sped immediately to the scene but had to be held off for several minutes while heavy debris continued to rain down into the ocean. At an altitude of nearly ten miles, the *Challenger*'s remains were falling over a wide area of the Atlantic Ocean.[117]

That night, President Ronald Reagan spoke to the nation: "I want to say something to the schoolchildren of America who were watching the live coverage of the shuttle's takeoff. I know it is hard to understand, but sometimes, painful things like this happen. It's all part of the process of exploration and discovery .... The future doesn't belong to the fainthearted; it belongs to the brave ...." Then he concluded, "We will never forget them [the crew], nor the last time we saw them, this morning, as they prepared for the journey, and waved goodbye, and slipped the surly bonds of earth to touch the face of G-d."

For many Americans, the *Challenger* disaster was a life-altering event, as the assassination of President Kennedy was for an older generation. Many remember where they were and what they were doing when they witnessed or heard about the explosion. For many

Jews, the disaster was a call to find the deeper message, and many sought an answer in that week's Torah portion, *parashas Yisro*.[118]

• Boundaries and the Beyond

Parashas Yisro is the *parashah* of *Matan Torah*, when *Hashem* revealed Himself to millions of people in the most awesome display of power recorded anywhere in *Tanach* (Scriptures):

> And it came to pass, on the third day[119] in the morning, that there were thunders and lightnings, and a thick cloud upon the mount, and the sound of a *shofar* exceedingly loud; so that all the people who were in the camp trembled .... And Mount Sinai was altogether in smoke, because *Hashem* descended upon it in fire; and its smoke ascended as the smoke of a furnace, and the whole mount trembled greatly. (*Shemos* 19:16-18)

Obviously, the man-made power of a rocket ship soaring into space cannot be measured against the awesome Presence and power of *Hashem* Himself. However, a shuttle take-off is certainly one of the most awe-inspiring displays that human hands have engineered. Observers invariably describe the spectacle as a most breathtaking sight, often employing adjectives similar to the Torah's description of the experience at Sinai (such as "thunder," "lightning," "heavy cloud," "extremely loud blast," "roar," "rumble," "tremble," etc.).

Naturally, this is not to suggest a comparison between a G-d-made and man-made event. Yet, that very similarity leads to the first obvious lesson of the *Challenger*: Be careful *not* to compare man-made to G-d-made! If one is not careful, one can blur the line between the acts of *Hashem* and man-made imitations. One might, G-d forbid, even *replace* in his mind the G-d-made with the man-made.

> "And you shall set bounds to the people around, saying, 'Take heed to yourselves, that you go not up onto the mount, or touch its border; whoever touches the mount shall be

surely put to death. There shall not a hand touch it, but he shall surely be stoned, or shot through; whether it be beast or man, it shall not live ....'" (*Shemos* 19:11-13)

The greater heights we scale, the greater the danger that we may lose ourselves and forget the great distance separating the human from the Divine. Therefore, in preparation for the revelation at Sinai, *Hashem* instructed Moshe to warn the people that despite the spiritual heights they were about to ascend, they should never forget how remote *Hashem's* greatness actually was from them.

The second lesson can be found in President Reagan's romantic description of the shuttle mission as an attempt to "touch the face of G-d." While this comment certainly wasn't made with the arrogance displayed by U.S.S.R. Cosmonaut Gherman Titov (He had triumphantly announced upon his return from orbiting the Earth in 1961 that he hadn't seen G-d. At the time, someone quipped, "Had he stepped out of his space-suit, he would have!"), it still indicates a lack of reverence and awe. One who follows the Torah is always aware that we cannot "touch" *Hashem* or His face—not literally, nor even figuratively.

> "As the heavens are higher than the earth, so are My ways higher than your ways and My thoughts than your thoughts." (*Yeshayahu* 55:9)

America generally does not evince the arrogance of atheistic communist Russia. But as leader of the arms race, as well as the space race, during that decade, she had positioned herself to become the world's sole superpower. With Reagan's grandiose "Star Wars" initiative[120] and the intended record-setting fifteen missions planned for the shuttle that year, America was definitely beginning to strut and swagger. If America—or only its leader, President Reagan—had the temerity to imagine it could even figuratively "touch the face of G-d," then what it needed was a good slap in the face. The *Challenger* disaster was just that.

A remarkable parallel to Reagan's statement about touching the face of G-d is the second of the Ten Commandments, which reads: "And you shall have no other gods [or "powers"] before *My face*"! Which leads us to a third lesson, an important lesson about faith in *Hashem*: It is not enough just to believe that *Hashem* exists (the first of the Ten Commandments). One must also rid from one's mind any idea that other powers or channels through which *Hashem* chooses to work have any real capabilities.[121]

This idea is well-illustrated by a story that took place in sixteenth century Safed (Tzfas).

• Don't Believe in Donkeys[122]

One of the legendary holy men in Tzfas was Rabbi Moshe Alshich, the Alshich Hakadosh ("the Holy Alshich"). An unsophisticated Jew heard the Alshich say that if one completely trusted in *Hashem*, his income would be delivered to his door. Now, this man worked excruciatingly hard every day. He would take his donkey up to the mountains, dig sand, put it in sacks, hoist them onto the back of the donkey and return to town to try to sell the sandbags. He barely made enough money to feed himself and his wife, not to mention his donkey.

The words of the holy rabbi inspired him, however, and he decided to sell his donkey business to an Arab. When he came home, his wife asked him why he was home so early.

"The rabbi said that if I have complete faith in *Hashem*, our income would be delivered to our door. So I sold the donkey."

"You *what?* That was all we had!"

"Well, here's the money from the sale. Use it until it runs out. Then *Hashem* will provide. Meanwhile, I am going to say *Tehillim* (Psalms) the whole day." (He was too unlearned to study Torah; reading Psalms was all he could do.)

So off went the man to a mound not far from his little shack, where he sat down and began reciting *Tehillim*, as his wife stared in disbelief.

Eventually, their money ran out and his wife complained, "What shall we do? We have no money. We have no donkey."

"Yes," the man replied. "Aren't we lucky we sold the donkey? Otherwise, we'd have to feed it, too."

Meanwhile, one day, the Arab who had purchased the donkey was digging sand when his shovel struck something hard and metallic. It was a chest. He dug it out, opened it and couldn't believe what his eyes saw—treasure beyond his imagination: gold, rubies, diamonds. He was set for life. He quickly loaded the treasure chest on the donkey and prepared to leave. Suddenly, a boulder came loose, rolled down the mountain and killed him.

The donkey stood waiting for a while. Eventually, not knowing what else to do, it started down the old trail it had traversed all the years before it had been sold to the Arab. Soon it arrived at the Jew's home.

The wife was the first to see it. When she opened the chest and saw the treasure, she almost fainted. Unable to contain her excitement, she ran to her husband, faithfully saying *Tehillim* on the mound.

"Treasure," she stammered. "There's a chest full of treasure and it just showed up at our door!"

Without batting an eyelash, her husband said matter-of-factly, "So? If the Holy Alshich said *Hashem* would take care of us, why are you surprised?" He then turned around and continued saying *Tehillim*.

Another Jew living in Tzfas heard this story. He had a donkey business of his own and figured if a simpleton like that other Jew could do it, he certainly could. He decided to sell his business and spend the entire day learning Torah.

A week went by.

Then a few more weeks …

Then a few months ...

But—no donkey arrived with treasure.

Finally, when the last of his provisions ran out and there was no relief in sight, he approached the Alshich and asked why *Hashem* had not provided him with an income as He had for the other Jew.

"Tell me the truth," the Alshich said. "While you were learning in the *yeshiva*, if you heard a noise outside, did you run to the window and look for the donkey?"

"Yes."

"You see," the Alshich smiled sadly. "You never relied on *Hashem*. You relied on the donkey."

❖ ❖ ❖

Consciously or subconsciously, we tend to invest great faith in the vehicles through which *Hashem* works—like our job, the state of the economy, technology and so on. The *Challenger* was a bigger "donkey." It symbolized humanity's over-reliance on a vehicle through which *Hashem* works: technology. There's nothing inherently wrong with technology, or any vehicle through which *Hashem* works. However, when people look to the "donkey" for sustenance, deliverance, worthiness or happiness, rather than to *Hashem*, it becomes an impediment to progress. Therefore, placing all our dependence on today's satellites to ensure our safety, etc., through a GPS or a cell phone, can lead—G-d forbid—to our forgetting the second commandment.

"You shall have no other gods before My face." It's not enough to believe in *Hashem* and just give lip service to the concept. There is no power—no god—except *Hashem*. Everything that transpires, whether tragic or magic, comes about because He so wills it. If we remember that then we can benefit from the "donkey." However, if it's the "donkey" we wait upon, we will wait upon it in vain.

The *Challenger* disaster was a great wake-up call to a nation and a world that was teetering on the brink of over-reliance upon the "donkey" of technological advancement. It was not the first such lesson, but it was a very powerful one for the twentieth century. However, as civilization continues to advance and forgets about this lesson, we put ourselves into the danger of having to learn it again, in—G-d forbid—a frightening, powerful and costly way.[123]

• Who Are We? And Who Are We in Relation to *Hashem*?

Belief in *Hashem*, which is the cornerstone of the Ten Commandments [and the entire Torah], is the true secret to "life, liberty and the pursuit of happiness." As we strive upwards toward our goals, we must never forget the lesson of humility, for whatever we accomplish, we are still not the makers of our own success. More than anything else, our occupation and position tend to draw us away from the raw truth of our being. They gain us money, status, power and even identity. But who are we, really? A doctor? A lawyer? A Rabbi? We create, and live in a world of "Image": name making, power plays and illusion. But who are we? Are we our bank account, career, connections, position?

An incident in Communist U.S.S.R. illustrates this poignantly. A religious Jew was incarcerated in Siberia, the slave-labor camp in northern Russia, during Stalin's "Reign of Terror." No matter what he was ordered to do, or how little he had to eat, or how painfully frostbitten he was, he never stopped singing his favorite *nigunim* (tunes) with joy and enthusiasm. A non-religious Jew raged at him in frustration, "What do you have to be happy about? You are a prisoner and a slave; you're starving; and you've been beaten today. These Russians think you're a piece of garbage! How can you sing?"

The frail little Jew stopped humming and turned sober. "Tell me," he said. "What were you before you came here?'

"I?" snorted the heretic. "Why, I was a distinguished doctor! What were you?"

"Ah," sighed his fellow Jew. "That's what makes you sad. You see, you are nothing here, when you were once a doctor. I, on the other hand, used to be an *eved Hashem* (servant of *Hashem*). And here, I am still an *eved Hashem*." He spread his hands and shrugged. "So—nothing has changed for me. I am still who I am. That's why I can sing." He closed his eyes, leaned back and resumed his *nigun*.

The Revelation at Sinai informs us of who we really are. Or, perhaps—who we are *not*; we are not *Hashem*. We have our limits. Regardless of our position in life, we are always lower than *Hashem* and are here to serve Him. Even the greatest human being has borders and boundaries, and is powerless to breach them.

Yet, when we humbly accept our boundaries and open ourselves to *Hashem*, His power surges through us and moves us to places we have never been before, beyond what we thought we could do. We are, perhaps, a metaphorical space shuttle, with millions of pounds of thrust driving us toward the heavens—not to challenge *Hashem* or "touch His face," but to hear, live up to and ultimately become living, amplified expressions of the word He spoke on Sinai.

• Shuttle Facts

✦ The Wright brothers' "Flyer" of 1903 weighed 605 pounds and traveled about 120 feet at approximately 40 mph. The space shuttle in 1986 weighed 4.5 million pounds and orbited the Earth as high as 400 miles at a speed of more than 17,000 mph. All that progress in only eighty-three years![124]

✦ Plans for NASA's Space Shuttle program were initially drafted in the late 1960s, when the objective of the Apollo program, to land a man on the moon, was about to be achieved. The original purpose of the program was to create a fleet of reusable vessels to ferry supplies to a large space station, which in turn would serve as a way-station for a permanently manned colony on the Moon, as well as an eventual manned mission to Mars. Budget cuts curtailed NASA's plans, but the shuttle program was given a green light on January 5, 1972, by President Richard Nixon.

+ The Six U.S. Shuttles:
  + *Enterprise*—test vehicle only suitable for glide/landing tests:
  + *Atlantis*
  + *Discover*
  + *Endeavour*

  Lost in accidents:
  + *Challenger*
  + *Columbia*

+ Shuttle Statistics
  + Space shuttle height: 184 feet
  + Orbiter alone: 122 feet long
  + Wingspan: 78 feet
  + Weight at liftoff: 4.5 million pounds
  + Weight at end of mission: 230,000 pounds
  + Maximum cargo to orbit: 63,500 pounds
  + Velocity: 17,321 mph

+ Each shuttle is designed for a projected lifespan of 100 launches. In January 2004, it was announced that the shuttle fleet would be replaced by 2010.

+ The first complete shuttle was to be called the *Constitution*. However, a massive write-in campaign from fans of the TV show "Star Trek" convinced the White House to change the name to *Enterprise*, after the interstellar vessel of that science fiction series.

+ *Enterprise* was rolled out on September 17, 1976, and later conducted a very successful series of landing tests, which was the first real validation of the gliding abilities of the design.

* The first fully functional shuttle orbiter was the *Columbia*, which was delivered to Kennedy Space Center on March 25, 1979. It was first launched on April 12, 1981, with a crew of two. The *Columbia* was lost with all seven crew, including Israeli astronaut Ilan Ramon, in a re-entry mishap on February 1, 2003.

* Although initial projections predicted a cost of $10 to $20 million per flight, in actual reality, each flight has cost approximately $500 million! During the 1970s, the U.S. suffered the worst inflation in modern history, driving up costs about 200% by 1980. (In contrast, the rate between 1990 and 2000 was only 34% in total.)

* The *Challenger* had flown nine successful missions before that fateful day in 1986.

* A special commission was appointed by President Ronald Reagan to investigate the cause of the accident. They found that the explosion of the $1.2 billion spacecraft was due to a seal on the solid rocket fuel booster, a $900 synthetic rubber band that engineers had warned was vulnerable at temperatures below 51 degrees. The launch of the *Challenger* had been canceled three times, finally taking place in 36-degree weather. These two rubber "O-rings" were supposed to remain flexible but had become hard and brittle due to the cold temperatures.

* In December 1986, the families of Christa McAuliffe, Ellison Onizuka, Gregory Jarvis and Dick Scobee accepted about $7.7 million from the U.S. and Morton Thiokol, the company that manufactured the rubber rings. The unrevealed sums designated for each family were based on the age and number of dependents of the deceased. The families of Ronald McNair and Judith Resnick sued Morton Thiokol and settled independently more than a year later, reportedly for multiple millions. The last suit to be resolved was that of Jane Smith, who, on the second

anniversary of the *Challenger* accident, filed a $1.5 billion suit against Morton Thiokol. "No one in big business should be allowed to make a faulty product and profit from it," she said. Her suit was settled for an undisclosed sum in 1988, just before the shuttle resumed flying ....

Portents of
Armageddon

OVERVIEW

"I heard in London from the holy Rabbi Elchanan
Wasserman, quoting the Chofetz Chaim, that
Chazal say the war of Gog and Magog will be threefold.
After the First World War, the Chofetz Chaim said
that this was the first battle of Gog and Magog, and in
about twenty-five years there would be a second world war,
which would make the first one seem insignificant,
and then there would be a third battle ...."

(RABBI ELIYAHU LOPIAN, LEV ELIYAHU, SHEMOS, P. 172)

The word "armageddon," derived from Mount (*Har* in Hebrew) Megiddo, the site of the Battle of Megiddo and other battles, refers in various theologies to an end-of-the-world scenario, usually a battle pitting the forces of good against the forces of evil. In *Tanach*, the ultimate conflict between light and darkness, between good and evil, is referred to by the prophets as *Milchemes Gog Umagog*, the "War of Gog and Magog" (e.g., Ezekiel, Chapter 38).[125] Before *Mashiach* (the Messiah) triumphs, the armies of Gog and Magog will join war against Israel. It will be a terrifying time, but Gog and Magog will be vanquished, and the long foretold era of peace among nations will be ushered in.[126]

The terrifying prospect of Armageddon reached new meaning with the onset of the Atomic Age, which was ushered in with World War II. The ensuing Cold War between the U.S. and the U.S.S.R., and the proliferation of nuclear technology, struck fear in the hearts of people around the world. Children growing up in the 1950s and '60s had practice drills at school in preparation of a nuclear attack. During the thirteen days in October 1962 known as the Cuban Missile Crisis, the world teetered at the edge of destruction. And the Gulf War in 1991 threatened to ignite global passions and set off a nuclear Armageddon.

The Sages explained how the era ushering in *Mashiach* will be so fraught with terror that, despite longing for his arrival, they exclaimed, "Let him come, but let me not be there." Nobody alive knows the details of the End-of-Days but perhaps we can become better prepared to deal with them as we examine the rich mine of Torah lessons in the critical events of the past century, and try to analyze and understand what may have been happening behind the scenes.

Hiroshima

A giant column of smoke rises more than 20,000 feet in the air after the second atomic bomb ever used in warfare explodes over the Japanese port of Nagasaki on August 9, 1945. The bomb killed more than 70,000 people instantly, with tens of thousands more dying later from effects of the radioactive fallout. This photo was taken three minutes after the atom bomb struck. (AP Photo/USAF)

"Behold, I will send you Eliyahu Hanavi before the coming of the great and terrible day of Hashem; And he shall turn the heart of the fathers to the children, and the heart of the children to their fathers, lest I come and destroy the Earth completely."

(MALACHI 3:23-24)

Colonel Paul Tibbets steadied the wheel of the *Enola Gay*, his B-29 bomber, as he circled above Hiroshima, a Japanese city with a population of 350,000. His plane carried only one bomb. It was 8:15 A.M., August 6, 1945.

Seventeen seconds later, the *Enola Gay's* bombardier took aim at a bridge, and pressed the release switch. The bomb dropped out of its belly, arcing downward.

The *Enola Gay* banked sharply in anticipation of the shock waves sure to follow the blast. A few long seconds passed and then a bright light filled the plane, noticed by each crewmember despite the fact that they were wearing special goggles to protect their eyes and were 30,000 feet in the sky!

About 2,000 feet above Hiroshima, the bomb had exploded like a huge flashbulb. Those directly below the blast simply vanished, leaving behind vague white shadows on blackened sidewalks (shadows that remained visible for years afterward).

After the initial flash, an eerie, bluish-green glow illuminated the sky all around. Then a thunderous shock wave followed, with a tremendous blast, followed in rapid succession by several more blasts resounding like cannon booms. It rattled the airship above from nose to tail, and crushed buildings below like toothpicks in the hands of a giant. People were buried in their homes, schools and workplaces.[127] Sheets of flame whipped through the city. Huge

Hiroshima

drops of black water the size of marbles began to fall. There was a strong odor of ionization, an electric smell given off by the bomb's fission. When the dust finally settled, an area of three square miles was completely leveled, except for a few reinforced concrete walls.

For a several long moments, everyone was silent.

Tibbets peered out the window. Prepared as he thought he was, he couldn't believe his eyes. "The surface was nothing but a black, boiling barrel of tar," he later noted.

Out of that boiling cauldron, "A giant ball of fire rose, as though from the bowels of the earth, belching forth enormous white smoke rings," one observer later wrote.[128] "A giant pillar of purple fire, moving upward with enormous speed," followed. Barely forty-five seconds after the blast, the purple fire rose to 30,000 feet, the height of the airship.

The pillar of fire and smoke—changing colors rapidly—rose in a perfectly straight column. Then, suddenly, "there came shooting out of the top, a giant mushroom, increasing the pillar's height to a total of forty-five thousand feet. The mushroom top was even more alive than the pillar, seething and boiling in a white fury of creamy foam, sizzling upward and then descending earthward, a thousand Old Faithful geysers rolled into one."[129]

Perhaps the most eloquent summation of the event was that of co-pilot Captain Robert Lewis, who said, "My G-d. What have we done?"

The Atomic Age had officially begun.

• The Ghastly Details

John Hersey, in *Hiroshima*, his account of the bombing, vividly describes the nightmare of the victims on the ground:

> "Shocked survivors seemed to be sleepwalking through
> the wreckage ... Eyebrows of some were burned off and skin
> hung from their faces and hands. Some were vomiting as

they walked. Many were ... in shreds of clothing. On some bodies, the burns had made patterns—of undershirt straps and suspenders [or of] the shapes of flowers they had had on their kimonos. Almost all had their heads bowed, looked straight ahead, were silent and showed no expression whatever .... The hurt ones were quiet; no one wept, much less screamed in pain ... none of the many who died did so noisily; not even the children cried ..."

It's estimated that at least 70,000 people lost their lives instantly in Hiroshima. Approximately another 70,000 were injured. Perhaps worst of all was the death and suffering cause by the radioactive fallout of the bomb.

"Hours after the atomic-bomb blast, Hiroshima was a city of dead and dying people. Many hospitals had been destroyed. The doctors and nurses who had survived set up aid stations on the outskirts of the city. Toward evening, doctors noticed puzzling things happening to the wounded. They began vomiting and having diarrhea. Many coughed up blood. Others were struck by a high fever. Their hair fell out in clumps. Red, green, and purple spots broke out on their skin. And they died. Many whose wounds did not seem severe, died for unexplained reasons.

"Scientists would later discover that radiation sickness was a deadly side effect of the atomic bomb. Inventors of the bomb had not guessed that their weapon would cause such awful sickness. Along with the fireball and the shock wave, the atomic bomb had released undreamed-of poisons that produced illnesses no doctor knew how to treat. Days, weeks, and years after the bomb exploded, its victims died."

Between 1946 and 1951, over 60,000 people died from radiation-related illnesses of the Hiroshima blast. The numbers from the Nagasaki blast were slightly smaller but still ghastly.

✦ ✦ ✦

The world changed irrevocably on August 6, 1945. Four years later, the Russians successfully tested their own atomic bomb, and the arms race was on. Both the U.S. and Russia began pouring money into the manufacture of newer and more lethal nuclear weapons. Within a couple of decades, each side had accumulated hundreds ... then thousands ... then tens of thousands of nuclear warheads, *hundreds of times* more powerful than the originals. The world had moved to the edge of self-annihilation.

Today, with the prospect of such weapons falling into the hands of modern terrorists, no one is safe. Every conscious human being in our post-atomic world is aware of, and fears, the possibility of actual, total annihilation.

• The Coming Of Eliyahu

Today's world is a different world—yet, it was foreseen long, long ago, echoed in the last words spoken by the last living *navi* (prophet):

"Behold, I will send you Eliyahu Hanavi before the coming of the great and terrible day of *Hashem*; And he shall turn the heart of the fathers to the children, and the heart of the children to their fathers, lest I come and destroy the Earth *completely.*" (*Malachi* 3:23-24)

✦ The Hebrew word for "completely," *chairem*, means "total," i.e., total destruction.

In the eighteenth century, the Vilna Gaon wrote that in the future, the human race would have the power to destroy itself in a matter of minutes.[130] In the twentieth century, this vision became true. The atom bomb, which ended World War II, gave the world something even more horrific: the ability to destroy hundreds of thousands of people instantly, with a single bomb.

• Two Trees, One Root

"And *Hashem* made grow from the ground every tree that is

pleasing to the sight and good for food; and the Tree of Life in the middle of the garden, and the Tree of Knowledge of Good and Evil." (*Bereishis* 2:9)

The Ramban (Nachmanides) expounds on the words "in the middle of the garden," stating that "both trees were in the middle." He (and others) believed that the Torah felt it necessary to emphasize this point because our normal perception is that there can only be one middle. Two objects cannot share the exact center. Either one is in the middle or the other. The Tree of Life and the Tree of Knowledge of Good and Evil were different, however. Both co-existed in one middle, one point.

In an allegorical sense, the Torah is relating a general principle of universal proportions. The description suggests one root, from which spring two trees—one branching off to a tree representing life, the other branching off to a tree representing death. We human beings are created with free will and must utilize our power of choice, forking off to either the side of life or the side of death. But there is nothing intrinsically good and nothing intrinsically bad about the root. Only how man relates to it makes it a tree of life or a tree of death.

This gift *Hashem* bestowed upon humanity—a gift of mind and spirit, to help His creations achieve a better life through their own efforts—i.e., to partake of the Tree of Life—is given the name "Science." The time-immemorial problem of humanity, however, is that it impetuously partakes of the Tree of Knowledge *before* the Tree of Life. It pursues knowledge without restraint, without subjugating it under the dictates of "Life," of what's ultimately good for life and for the living. Knowledge without morals is a recipe for death. This was the first human's mistake, the Torah tells us. And it's a lesson humanity has apparently yet to learn.

Many of the scientists whose ideas and/or expertise helped create the atom bomb were secular Jews (including Einstein, Oppenheimer, Szilard and Fermi). Some of Europe's most brilliant minds were refugees from Hitler's death machine, and believed that they were helping the Allies acquire this deadly weapon before the Nazis. When they found out that the Nazis had not had the bomb, many regretted their participation, feeling tremendous guilt in having played a key part in something that could eventually annihilate humanity.

Chazal tell us: "Marbeh talmidei chachamim, marbeh shalom— The more Torah scholars, the more peace." Knowledge is a two-edged sword. It's a Tree of Life or a Tree of Death. Too late, those scientists realized their efforts had created a Tree of Death. Ironically, the brilliance and renown that had enabled them to flee death and live was put to a dastardly use—enabling other humans to cause death and suffering on a scale never before seen.

The navi tells us that we are to be a "light unto the nations." The lesson of the atomic bomb demonstrates that if we are to be a light, it must be a spiritual light—the light of Torah, not the fearsome, eerie light unleashed in a physical, nuclear blast. We must place the Tree of Life before the Tree of Knowledge, for without the guiding light of Torah, the Tree of Knowledge will surely turn to a Tree of Death.

This concept was unwittingly echoed in a statement by a non-Jewish American general: "We have too many men of science, too few men of G-d ...," said General Omar Bradley, Chief-of-Staff of the U.S. Army in World War II. "The world has achieved brilliance without wisdom, power without conscience. Ours is a world of nuclear giants and ethical infants. We know more about war than we know about peace, more about killing than we know about living."

• Additional Atomic Facts

+ As the Enola Gay dropped the bomb on August 6, Truman was aboard a cruiser on his way back to the United States. After receiving the news, he made a radio speech announcing that a new and powerful bomb had obliterated Hiroshima. He added that if the Japanese did not surrender, they could expect, "a rain of ruin from the air, the like of which had never been seen on this earth." Incredibly, Japanese military leaders decided to fight on rather than surrender. On August 8, the Soviet Union attacked the Japanese army occupying China. Truman and the Americans expected this, but the Japanese, who had signed a Neutrality Pact with Stalin, did not. Yet, even then, they did not surrender. On August 9, three days after the first bomb, another was dropped on the city of Nagasaki, instantly killing some 40,000 people. Japan had received overwhelming body-blows. Yet, after two atomic bombings, massive conventional bombings and the Soviet invasion, the Japanese government still refused to surrender.[131] It wasn't until August 14 that they accepted American terms, and then only after an unprecedented intervention by their emperor.

✦ In 1945, the Japanese still held about 400,000 Allied prisoners of war in Japan and other territories. These POWs had been tortured, killed, used as slave labor and poorly fed, and were being slowly starved to death; many had only a few months to live. It is interesting to note that 4% of all U.S. POWs held by the Germans died in captivity, while 28% of our POWs held by the Japanese died in captivity. An order had been issued by the Japanese to execute all POWs when the home islands were invaded. This had already begun in some of the Philippine POW camps.

✦ The code-name of the secret program to build the atomic bomb was the "Manhattan Project," which involved 200,000 people working night and day for three years. It resulted in the creation of two fundamentally different bombs, a uranium one and a plutonium one. The former worked like a gun. A piece of uranium was fired into another piece of uranium at extremely high velocity. This created a critical mass, exploding the atoms and releasing their energy. This, in turn, created a chain reaction that released more and more energy. The problem was that uranium, a natural substance, was difficult to come by. Plutonium, on the other hand, was a man-made substance that was relatively easy to produce. The plutonium bomb worked very differently than the uranium one. Rather than creating a chain reaction via an *explosion*, it did so via an *implosion*. A core of plutonium the size of a grapefruit was compressed in upon itself by detonating explosives *around* it. The entire force was directed inward. This was a radical new design, and the scientists felt it was therefore imperative that the plutonium bomb be tested.

✦ The test took place on July 16, 1945 (6 Av), in a lonely area of the New Mexican desert. Most scientists believed the bomb would have an explosive force of between 1,000 and 2,000 tons of TNT. However, the first atomic bomb blew up with a force of 20,000 tons of TNT, exploding into a dazzling ball of orange light. Temperatures inside the ball were three times that of the sun. Desert sand beneath the blast melted and fused into glass. The 100-foot-tall steel tower that had held the test bomb vanished without a trace. The flash of light from the experiment was seen for more than ten miles. A soldier 10,000 feet away was knocked off his feet by the shock wave. Another soldier over five miles away was temporarily blinded. A girl in a town many miles away, who had been blind her entire life, saw a flash of light. The explosion was heard fifty miles away. J. Robert Oppenheimer, the scientist in overall charge of the project who had originally predicted the blast would produce the equivalent of 2,000 tons of TNT, realized that in a few years the military would have a thermonuclear device capable of unleashing the equivalent of 1,000,000 tons of TNT.

✦ "The atomic bomb made the prospect of future war unendurable.

It has led us up those last few steps to the mountain pass; and beyond there is a different country." —J. Robert Oppenheimer

+ "The physicists have known sin; and this is a knowledge which they cannot lose." —J. Robert Oppenheimer

+ "I made one great mistake in my life—when I signed that letter to President Roosevelt recommending that atom bombs be made, but there was some justification—the danger that the Germans would make them." —Albert Einstein

+ Not long before the bomb was first tested in New Mexico, Leo Szilard, one of the inventors of the bomb, tried frantically to get the test cancelled, as well as have the secret of the bomb buried. As long as the bomb hadn't been used, he argued, it was not too late to save civilization from the terrible arms race he saw coming. Szilard argued that until the test, no one would be certain it could be done. Russia was desolated and exhausted by the war. Stalin, the argument went, wouldn't waste his limited resources on an atomic weapon ... unless he knew it could be done. Unfortunately, the genie had already been let out of the bottle. Unbeknownst to Szilard, Truman and everyone else on the Allied side, Klaus Fuchs, one of the scientists developing the bomb, was passing its secrets on to the Russians.[132] The world, as Oppenheimer said, had already changed forever.

+ In 1933, Leo Szilard fled Germany for London to escape Nazi persecution. He read an article by eminent scientist Ernest Rutherford stating that "anyone who looked for a source of power in the transformation of the atoms was talking moonshine." Walking through the streets of central London after reading this article, he conceived the idea of creating a chain reaction.

+ In 1934, Enrico Fermi, then at the University of Rome, began bombarding uranium with neutrons in an attempt to split it and release its energies. His experiments were successfully applied in the fall of 1938, when scientists Otto Hahn and Fritz Strassman, at the Kaiser Wilhelm Institute of Berlin in Nazi Germany, split the uranium atom.

✦ Szilard and two fellow Jewish refugees (Eugene Wigner and Edward Teller) in the U.S. had kept up with what was happening abroad through letters from old friends—Jews mostly, who had been driven out of Germany to Belgium, Britain and Sweden. By the winter of 1938/9, the three began to hear that the Germans were working on something called the "uranium problem." They then received a letter from Lise Meitner, a German Jewish physicist who had fled from Hitler and was now in Sweden. She told them something that would have meant nothing to the State Department: Germany had suddenly banned all exports of uranium ore from Czechoslovakia. Szilard and his two friends were the only people in the United States who were alarmed by this news. They felt they had to warn somebody. The problem was that they were unknown refugees. No one would listen to them. Suddenly they thought of an old man who might be able to help. In what can only be described as a comedy, Szilard and Wigner—these two eccentric Jewish immigrants—woke one morning and got out a map of Long Island. They knew that the old man had rented a cottage for the summer from a Dr. Moore—that's all. So, on a drenching hot midsummer day, they set out in search of the old man renting a cottage in some town with an Indian-sounding name that started with a "P". Long Island is 120 miles long and choked with Indian-sounding names; they first traveled all the way out to Patchogue before realizing that the town they were looking for was Peconic. When they finally found the old man, he greeted them in his slippers. (They were lucky he was home, because he often spent many hours alone in a little sailboat.) The old man was Albert Einstein. They convinced Einstein to draft a letter that changed history.

+ Albert Einstein, the world's most renowned scientist, was not directly involved in the Manhattan Project. However, a letter he sent to the president in 1939 eventually sparked Roosevelt to act (see below). His famous Special Theory of Relativity postulated that a relatively large amount of energy was contained in, and could be released from, a relatively small amount of matter. This became best known by the equation $E=MC^2$. The atomic bomb was not based upon this theory, however, even while it clearly illustrated the potential.

+ Einstein wrote the letter to President Roosevelt on August 2, 1939, one month before the outbreak of World War II. It read: "Some recent work of E Fermi and L Szilard which has been communicated to me in manuscript leads me to expect that the element uranium may be turned into a new and important source of energy in the immediate future. Certain aspects of the situation which has arisen seem to call for watchfulness and if necessary, quick action on the part of the administration. I believe, therefore, it is my duty to bring to your attention the following facts and recommendations. In the course of the last four months, it has been made probable, through the work of Joliet in France, as well as Fermi and Szilard in America, that it may become possible to set up a nuclear chain reaction in a large mass of uranium by which vast amounts of power and large quantities of new radium-like elements would be generated, by which, my dear Mr. President, it might be possible to unleash an immense destructive force." Through a banker, who knew another banker, who had an acquaintanceship with the president, the letter got to Roosevelt two months later. Other than jotting down a quick note, Roosevelt did nothing ... until just after Pearl Harbor. At that time, he remembered Einstein's letter and set in motion the $2 billion "Manhattan Project" that produced the bomb.

+ Despite the devastating effects of the atom bomb, the bombing of Tokyo in March 1945—by more than 300 B-29s dropping napalm incendiary bombs—did more damage. The Tokyo raid killed between 80-100,000, wounded the same amount and wiped out an area of nearly sixteen square miles (as opposed to three square miles at Hiroshima).

+ A tragic event occurred to the USS *Indianapolis*, the American ship that delivered the bomb to Tinian Island, where the *Enola Gay* took off on its fateful mission a few days later. After unloading the bomb, the *Indianapolis* sailed off for operations in the Philippines. However, the unescorted cruiser (unescorted because its mission was top-secret) was torpedoed four days later, and the ship went down without even sending an SOS. Three days passed before Pearl Harbor's naval nerve center realized that *Indianapolis* was overdue. As a result, the 800 who managed to abandon ship spent a grueling eighty-four hours in the sea, facing thirst, fatigue and, worst of all, sharks. When help at last arrived, only 316 of the *Indianapolis's* total crew of 1,200 were picked up alive.

+ In the morning of August 6, 1945, there was great tension as Colonel Paul Tibbets taxied the *Enola Gay* into a take-off position. Just the day before, *four* overloaded B-29s had crashed while trying to take off. If an accident occurred with the atomic bomb on board, the entire island base could be wiped out! Therefore, navy weapons expert Captain William Parsons insisted on a last-minute change in plans: Instead of arming the bomb before take-off, he would arm it in flight. Nevertheless, no one was sure what would happen in the event of a crash. So, as Tibbets raced his bomber down the runway, everyone held their breath. Even at 180 miles an hour— usually fast enough to lift a plane into the air—the great weight of the bomb still held it down. Finally, with just a few feet of runway left, the B-29 lifted off the airstrip.

✦ "Does one feel any pity or compassion for the poor devils about to die? Not when one thinks of Pearl Harbor and of the Death March on Bataan." William L. Laurence, writing on board a B-29 about to drop the atomic bomb on Nagasaki: "A Thousand Old Faithful Geysers Rolled into One Blast"; *The New York Times*, September 9, 1945.

The
Cuban Missile
Crisis

This photo shows Soviet missile equipment being loaded at the Mariel naval port in Cuba on November 5, 1962. (AP Photo/U.S. Department of Defense)

"A time of trouble such as has never been seen."

(DANIEL 12:1)

"**T**his was not only the most dangerous moment of the Cold War. It was the most dangerous moment in human history." (Arthur Schlesinger, Kennedy aide and historian)

October 22, 1962. 7:00 P.M. (EST).

Amid rumors of U.S. troop mobilization and rumors of something big amiss, President John F. Kennedy appears on national television:

"Good evening, my fellow citizens: This Government, as promised, has maintained the closest surveillance of the Soviet military buildup on the island of Cuba. Within the past week, unmistakable evidence has established the fact that a series of offensive missile sites is now in preparation on that imprisoned island. The purpose of these bases can be none other than to provide a nuclear strike capability against the Western Hemisphere ... [The missiles are] capable of carrying a nuclear warhead for a distance of more than 1,000 nautical miles. Each of these missiles, in short, is capable of striking Washington, D.C., the Panama Canal, Cape Canaveral, Mexico City, or any other city in the southeastern part of the United States, in Central America, or in the Caribbean area .... This urgent transformation of Cuba into an important strategic base by the presence of these large, long-range and clearly offensive weapons of sudden mass destruction constitutes an explicit threat to the peace and security of all the Americas ....

"It shall [therefore] be the policy of this Nation to regard any nuclear missile launched from Cuba against any nation in the Western Hemisphere as an attack by the Soviet Union on the United States, requiring a full retaliatory response upon the Soviet Union."

For the next week, the United States and the Soviet Union teetered on the brink of global nuclear war. Today, we know the outcome, for had it come to war, few if any of us would be here. Nevertheless, the emotion, tension, anguish, despair and terror of the event known today as the "Cuban Missile Crisis" knows no parallel. The world's superpowers were playing a game of high stakes that could easily have ended in the deaths of hundreds of millions of people, making World War II look tame by comparison.[133]

The roots of this conflict shed profound light upon the events of our own times and teach timely Torah lessons.

• The Iron Curtain

The U.S. and Soviet Union (U.S.S.R.) had led the fight to defeat Hitler, and famous photos like that of an American and Soviet soldier shaking hands near the Elbe River in defeated Germany were shown to the world as signature moments of the warm feelings between the two military giants. Before the war's end (at the Yalta Conference), "the big three"—Franklin Roosevelt, Winston Churchill and Joseph Stalin—had made agreements about how to cut up Europe. Stalin had agreed to withdraw from many of the lands his army fought hard for and eventually won. However, after the war, he failed to keep his promises. Poland, Hungary and other Eastern European countries were swept into the Soviet empire, under oppressive communist regimes.

By March 1946, Winston Churchill had summed up the situation: "From Stettin in the Baltic to Trieste in the Adriatic, an iron curtain has descended across the [European] Continent."

This "iron curtain" was the foundation of the Cold War.

• Bombs, Bombs & More Bombs

In 1949, the Soviet Union had conducted a test, exploding its first atomic bomb.[134] By 1953, shortly before Stalin's death, they exploded their first hydrogen bomb,[135] which was almost 500 times more powerful than the bomb that wiped out the Japanese city of Nagasaki. At the same time, intercontinental missiles capable of carrying nuclear warheads were built and perfected.

In 1957, the Soviets successfully launched the Sputnik satellite into space, creating a panic in the U.S. Besides indicating that the Soviet Union could build missiles capable of hitting anywhere in the world, Sputnik proved that they had pulled ahead of the U.S. in missile technology.[136] This realization sent shockwaves through the American psyche and helped escalate the nuclear arms race to the point of no return.[137]

Citizens in both countries braced themselves for World War III. Schools taught children civil defense, i.e., what to do in case of a nuclear attack. It went so far that even common homeowners built bomb shelters in their backyards. World War III, if it ever came, would be the "final war," the war no side could survive, no less win.

▫ Paranoia—Real & Perceived

When Soviet leader Josef Stalin died in 1953, Nikita Khrushchev took over. Khrushchev was considered by his enemies, both within and without the Soviet Union, to be boorish and uncouth. At a famous U.N. meeting, he removed his shoe and threatened to bang it on the table. Another time, he boastfully declared to the West, "We will bury you."[138] At that time, two million West Berliners were behind the "Iron Curtain," surrounded by Soviet armies. The only chance America had to hold off the Soviets was to threaten use of nuclear weapons if the Soviets advanced on West Berlin.

Khrushchev had to find a way to counter that threat with one of his own, since the Americans had great superiority in nuclear weapons and delivery systems. So he proceeded to engage in a game of cat-and-mouse, boasting that, "We are producing missiles like sausages," when in truth, he knew his arsenal lagged far behind the Americans.[139] If nothing else, however, the bluffing created paranoia in the American public and leadership.[140]

If the Soviet Union were to counter the U.S. threat credibly, they would have to find a closer launching point than Europe. Cuba seemed viable, as its dictator had recently been overthrown by a young, upstart revolutionary named Fidel Castro.

The Soviets built their relationship with Castro gradually. (Castro had actually been considered a hero at first in the eyes of much of the American public. Only later did it become obvious that he was surrounding himself with communists.) First, they sent him economic aid. Then they sent military aid and advisors. As the U.S. watched these developments, Castro fell quickly from the "idealistic revolutionary" to an extremely dangerous communist leader.

When Kennedy took office, he was presented a plan to oust Castro. The CIA secretly had helped train and arm a small army of around 1,400 Cuban exiles to invade Cuba and depose Castro. Kennedy immediately signed the plan into action, a mistake since it was filled with blunders. It was over two days after it began (April 17, 1961), with all the Cuban exiles slaughtered or captured (about 400 killed, 1,000 captured). History called this fiasco the "Bay of Pigs." Worst of all for the Americans, their involvement was exposed. It was a military disaster, and an even larger political one, for the young, new U.S. president.

In February 1962, the Soviets stepped up their military aid to Cuba, claiming that it was now necessary to protect Castro and that their military aid was only of a defensive nature, e.g., anti-aircraft guns and patrol boats. The U.S. watched this build-up but decided to tolerate it. However, they drew a line publicly and privately: Do what you feel is necessary. But don't put nuclear weapons in Cuba, or the gravest consequences will arise. The Soviets promised, publicly and privately, that they wouldn't cross that line.

• The Crisis

In the early morning hours of October 14, 1962, an American U-2 spy plane took reconnaissance pictures of Cuba from the air, revealing that nuclear missiles sites were set up on the island. The missiles were not yet operational, the photos showed, but the Soviets were making efforts to speed up their efforts and keep their activities secret.

President Kennedy was informed at once. When the missiles became operational, he was told, the cities and citizens of the U.S. would be threatened with annihilation. Indeed, a nuclear missile launched from Cuba could hit Washington, D.C. and other major cities within five minutes, killing as many as eighty million people! Never before had the U.S. been faced with such a threat. Never before had a U.S. president been faced with such a crisis.[141]

Kennedy chose to keep the information secret so he could plan a course of action before the momentum of the events forced him to act. His military advisors were suggesting a massive surprise attack on Cuba and the Soviet missile sites, followed by an all-out invasion by American forces. The problem with an invasion was that it would likely lead to an all-out war with the Soviets, which could easily become a nuclear holocaust. Kennedy's military could not assure him that they would destroy 100% of the missiles. And if the Russians had even one nuclear missile left to fire, it could wipe out millions of Americans.

Second, even if no nuclear missiles in Cuba were fired, Kennedy felt certain the Soviets would respond by invading West Berlin. West Berlin was to the U.S.S.R. what Cuba was to the U.S. If West Berlin were invaded, America was bound by treaty and other considerations to defend it. War, probably including nuclear weapons, would ensue.

The world was kept in the dark as Kennedy and his advisors debated the issue. Each day that passed meant the missiles were more nearly operational. And once they became operational, U.S.

military action became infinitely more dangerous.

Eventually, Kennedy decided on a risky measure: to blockade Cuba. He didn't use the term blockade because historically, a blockade is an act of war. Instead, he used the term "quarantine." He wanted to give the Soviets the chance to dismantle the missiles and pull out of Cuba. This was dangerous, and particularly dismaying to some military people, since it removed all possibility of a surprise attack. Once he announced the "quarantine," the Soviets would be on high alert against a U.S. military action.

However, he could not keep the secret forever. A few days into the crisis, the nation's leading newspapers got wind of the situation, and as they were about to publish the scoop, Kennedy jumped in ahead of them and addressed the nation himself.

• The Public Phase

Once the crisis became public, tension mounted. Neither side wanted war, but each felt cornered. On October 24, Soviet merchant ships (perhaps carrying more missiles) approached the blockade line. American naval warships confronted them. Suddenly, they detected a Soviet submarine.

Was this to begin the war?

Surprisingly, the Soviet ships stopped dead in the water. To quote one of Kennedy's advisors, "We were eyeball to eyeball and the other guy just blinked." Then, they simply turned around.

Nevertheless, the crisis wasn't over. On October 25, the U.S. military went into alert DEFCON 2, one level below all-out war.

• The Climax

The crisis peaked on October 27 (*Shabbos parashas Bereishis*). First, the missile sites in Cuba became operational; nuclear missiles were ready to be loaded onto their launch pads to be fired at the United States. Second, an American U-2 spy plane accidentally veered off course and wandered into Soviet air space. The pilot radioed he was lost, and the base promptly dispatched fighters armed with missiles containing nuclear warheads. At the same time, Soviet fighters scrambled to intercept the U-2, interpreting this as a final reconnaissance mission before a nuclear attack. Nuclear war could easily have ensued, but fortunately, the U-2 left Soviet air space before the two fighter groups met.

Later that day, however, another U-2 flew over Cuba to get updated pictures of the missile sites. It was shot down. Worse, its pilot was killed. When Robert McNamara, Secretary of Defense, heard the news, he turned white and proclaimed, "This means war ...."[142]

As Kennedy and his advisors debated their options, a letter arrived from Khrushchev demanding an American declaration that they never invade Cuba. He had sent a letter like this before, but now he added a second demand—the removal of U.S. nuclear missiles in Turkey as well. It was one thing to pledge never to invade Cuba. It was another to withdraw missiles from Turkey, thereby losing American credibility with her allies.

President Kennedy was in a terrible bind. If he did too little, he would embolden the Soviets. If he did too much, he would start World War III.

• The End

That night, Robert Kennedy, the president's thirty-five-year-old brother and Attorney General, secretly met with Soviet Ambassador Anatoly Dobrynin. He offered a deal that included a pledge not to invade Cuba, as well as the withdrawal of U.S. missiles from Turkey (if the latter was not announced publicly).[143] At the same time, however, he impressed upon the ambassador that if the U.S.S.R. did not accept the deal, the Americans would never let the missiles in Cuba remain—meaning, he intimated in the strongest possible terms, that time was just about out; the

Soviets must accept these terms immediately or action was imminent.

Robert Kennedy left the Soviet ambassador unsure of the effect he had had. He, and many others closest to the situation, expected to wake up next morning—if they woke up—in the grip of the "final war."

Sunday, October 28, dawned to the welcome news that Khrushchev had broadcast an announcement over Radio Moscow. The Soviets, he said, would dismantle their nuclear missiles in Cuba. Khrushchev could have insisted that the U.S. respond to the greater demands in the second letter, but he did not. War had been averted at the last moment.

• Comments on Kennedy

The way he handled the Cuban Missile Crisis is considered by many to be the high point of John F. Kennedy's presidency. He learned from the "Bay of Pigs" whom to trust, and how to employ his advisors in the decision-making process.[144] Kennedy based many of his decisions during the crisis on the poignant lessons in Barbara Tuchman's Pulitzer Prize-winning book *Guns of August*, about the underlying causes of World War I.

"World War I," he declared, "came about through a series of misjudgments of the intentions of others." The hard, unbending bone-headedness of the world's leaders at that time thrust upon humanity a bloody world war that conceivably could have been avoided.

World War II, on the other hand, evolved in part because appeasers like Neville Chamberlain gave into the demands of Hitler.[145] The pendulum had swung the other way; people with the power to oppose an aggressor were too soft.[146]

During the "Missile Crisis," Kennedy was abundantly aware of the thin line he was treading between an aggressive military stance and a yielding weakness in the face of aggressor. He had walked that line successfully, convincing the Soviets to remove the missiles, avoiding a nuclear war and maintaining U.S. credibility with her allies. (Khrushchev, by contrast, was eventually removed from office, mostly for his performance during the crisis.)

• A Hard Rain

To those attuned to the events and the weekly *parashah*, the timing of the Cuban Missile Crisis must have been particularly unnerving. As noted, the confrontation reached its climax on *Shabbos parashas Bereishis*. This *parashah* begins with the creation of the world, but ends with a *threat* of its destruction:

"*Hashem* said, 'I will obliterate humanity that I have created from the face of the earth—man, livestock, land animals and birds of the sky. I regret that I created them.'"

The world was *threatened* with destruction in 1962, just when we read the *parashah* where *Hashem* threatens this very thing. In *parashas Noach*, the world is destroyed. It's therefore perhaps more than lucky that the crisis did not boil over *even one day into the week* of the *parashah* in which the world was destroyed. The U.S. had plans to invade Cuba with a massive air strike followed by a ground invasion as early as Monday, October 29—*Rosh Chodesh Cheshvan* (the start of the month of Cheshvan), the month of the *Mabul* (the Flood). Plans had also been drawn up to position Polaris submarines armed with nuclear missiles off the shores of Turkey. Strategic Air Command had stepped up its readiness, sending scores of B-52 bombers armed with nuclear weapons toward Soviet airspace, scheduled to continue toward Soviet targets if need be.[147]

As the Chofetz Chaim taught, an earthquake on the other side of the world is meant for us to reflect and do *teshuva*. How much more so when the fate of the entire world hangs in the balance?

Although *Hashem* promised to never destroy the world again through a flood (9:11), there is no guarantee against destruction though fire, including fire from a nuclear holocaust.

The *navi* warns that before *Mashiach* arrives, the world will reach a point where all looks bleak—"Behold, I will send you Eliyahu Hanavi before the coming of the great and terrible day of *Hashem* ...." Nevertheless, that time of terrible travail will have one purpose: to cause *teshuva*—"And he shall turn the heart of the fathers to the children, and the heart of the children to their fathers, lest I come and destroy the Earth completely." (*Malachi* 3:23-24)

There is a rule that a prophecy foretelling good must come true, but a prophecy foretelling bad will not necessarily come to pass (*Rambam, Yesodei HaTorah* 10:4). It can be voided through *teshuva*. Cheshvan is a time to make a *cheshbon*, to take stock. It's the month to reflect on how humanity was once wiped out, and to recognize that although the event seems far away, it really is not. It's an important message to take to heart, especially given the volatile nature of our world today and the history of the not-too-distant past.

• Cuba Scoops

+ When Kennedy found out about the missiles, he immediately organized a committee, EX-COMM, a group of his twelve most important advisors, to handle the crisis. Khrushchev, in contrast, did not have any advisors to help him through the crisis. He spent many long, lonely hours in deliberation over what action to take about the United States' threat.

+ Poor communication contributed to the escalation of the Cuban Missile Crisis. In 1962, there was no direct and immediate link between the American and Soviet leaders. Once the crisis entered its public phase on October 22, Kennedy and Khrushchev used various written communiqués and television and radio speeches to negotiate with one another. This somewhat unreliable and indirect form of communication nearly led to nuclear war. Realizing how close they had come to disaster, Kennedy and Khrushchev established the "hot line" between the White House and the Kremlin after the crisis, so that they could speak directly.

+ "The blast of an atomic bomb, a fission weapon, had been calculated in kilotons, each kiloton equivalent to 1,000 tons of TNT. The blast of a hydrogen bomb, a fusion weapon, was calculated in megatons, each equivalent to 1,000 kilotons, or a million tons of TNT .... The bombs used against Hiroshima and Nagasaki had been huge, handcrafted devices, so delicate and so difficult to engineer that it had been hard to imagine their ever existing in large numbers. The Hiroshima bomb had been 10 feet long, weighed almost 5 tons, and, to be loaded in an airplane and armed to explode, required a crew of experts, working several days. By the time of the missile crisis, bombs twenty times more powerful were 3 feet long, shaped like ordinary TNT bombs, and easily slapped onto the wing of a ground-based or carrier-based fighter-bomber."[148]

+ "As of 1960 the actual nuclear arsenal of the United States was enormous. That of the Soviet Union, according to calculations by the U.S. intelligence community, was smaller but also huge ... When Eisenhower yielded the presidency to Kennedy, the United States would have around 18,000 nuclear weapons ... Though U.S. intelligence analysts doubted that the total Soviet arsenal yet matched America's, they had no question that the Soviets, too, possessed what critics already decried as 'overkill ... ' [enough] that there just might be nothing left of the Northern Hemisphere [if they used them]."[149]

+ An important catchword of the Cold War was "second strike." During the 1950s, some of the best minds in the world tried to untangle the logic of using nuclear weapons to defend territory, despite the likelihood that their actual use would obliterate the territory and be suicidal for the defender. One early insight was that a nuclear arsenal might not achieve any true deterrence— indeed, it might encourage both aggression and nuclear war—if it could be destroyed in a disarming first strike, for a state might be tempted to rid itself at once of resistance to its aggression and any danger of its own annihilation. It followed that a nuclear arsenal served as a deterrent if so configured that significant forces would survive any attempt at a disarming first strike. This "second strike" capability would guarantee the attacker's devastation, no matter what.[150]

+ Part of the "second strike" philosophy was the creation of the Strategic Air Command (SAC), squadrons of B-52 bombers carrying nuclear bombs. When put on alert, SAC would put approximately 180 bombers in the air *flying at all times.* Fully loaded with nuclear bombs, they would fly (often refueled in midair) to a preassigned line a certain distance from the Soviet Union and then, unless ordered to proceed, would turn around and fly back. At one point, SAC bombers deliberately flew past their turnaround points and only turned around when the Soviet freighters carrying the missiles to Cuba stopped dead in the Atlantic.

+ The Soviet Union never went to full nuclear alert all the years of the Cold War. After Cuba, the U.S. never did again either. Neither did the two nations ever directly confront each other again.

+ Fidel Castro was born near Mayari, Cuba, in 1926. In 1950, he graduated from the University of Havana with a law degree and opened a law office with two partners. Two years later, he ran for election to the Cuban House of Representatives. The elections were never carried out because then dictator

Fulgencio Batista halted them and ended democracy in Cuba. This was, perhaps, the defining moment in Castro's life. Castro immediately went into exile and began to train a group of revolutionaries called "The 26th of July Movement." Over the next two years, he gained increasing support from the Cuban people and on January 1, 1959, Batista fled the country. Shortly after Castro took control of the government, relations with the United States declined. In 1960, he took over U.S. oil refineries in Cuba. The U.S. then stopped buying Cuban sugar, and Castro responded by taking over all U.S. businesses in Cuba.

+ Nikita Khrushchev was born in 1894, the son of a miner. He spent his early years working as a shepherd and locksmith. After fighting in World War I, he joined the Communist party and the Red Army in 1918, and fought in the civil war. Khrushchev attended a Communist party high school in 1921 where he became active as a political organizer. Shortly thereafter, his rapid rise to power began.

The
Gulf War

A U.S. Marine patrol walks across the charred oil landscape near a burning
well during perimeter security patrol near Kuwait City on March 7, 1991.
(AP Photo/John Gaps III)

At the end of twelve months he [Nevuchadnezzar]
was walking upon the royal palace of Babylon.
The king spoke, and said: "Isn't this Babylon, which
I have built ... by the might of my power and
for the glory of my majesty, is it not great?" While the
word was in the king's mouth ... at that moment ...
Nevuchadnezzar [went mad and] ... was driven
from the world of men, ate grass as oxen, his body was
wet with the dew of heaven, his hair wild like an
eagles' feathers, and his nails like birds' claws."

(DANIEL 4:26-28, 30)

News of Saddam Hussein's capture on December 13, 2003 electrified the world. The man who had thumbed his nose at the West, who sat on the planet's second largest oil reserve and who had assembled the world's fourth largest army; the man who fancied himself a reincarnated version of the Babylonian world conqueror, Nevuchadnezzar, was discovered cowering in a coffin-like hole, dazed, confused, disheveled and looking something less than human.

This was the man ... the menace who had persuaded tens if not hundreds of thousands to die for the cause of his leadership; who was celebrated throughout his "kingdom" with numerous massive statues in heroic postures; and who surrendered to American troops, meekly as a lamb.

"Now, the question that presses on the angry men of Tikrit
and Ad Dwar is why their fallen idol failed to fight it out
with his captors, leaving a pistol and a Kalashnikov rifle lying

on the bunker floor as he emerged, hands raised, into the night.

"'It was a mistake to hide in such a disgusting place, a dishonor for Saddam, but also for Iraq,' said Hatim Jassem, 35, a theology professor. 'People saw him on television and said: "This is pathetic. He has disappointed us. He has let Iraq down."'"

—*New York Times*

+ ✦ +

Nothing happens by accident, especially events with global repercussions. Indeed, such events are loud messages. Of course, it's sheer arrogance to presume to understand the Divine Plan behind the historic moment as it occurs. But, armed with Torah, we have some ability, and indeed an obligation, to strive for a glimpse behind the curtain and find out just what the *yad Hashem* may be trying to tell us.

And, if so, it seems to me that the capture of Saddam is a telegram from *shamayim* (heaven), sent to remind us of the lessons of the Gulf War, which shares the same basic theme as the lesson of *Chanukah*.

• Ominous Beginnings

By the summer of 1990, Saddam had well established himself on a global scale as an archetypal tyrant. However, that summer, he added a new chapter to his infamy, a chapter that would include the Jewish People as one of its main characters. And, not surprisingly, the beginning of this chapter coincided with some of the most infamous dates on the Jewish calendar.

On July 17, 1990—the "Three Weeks" (24 Tammuz 5750)— Saddam Hussein appeared on Iraqi national TV and accused

Kuwait and the United Arab Emirates of overproduction of oil, thereby flooding the world market and decreasing the income from his sole export.

On August 1, 1990—the tenth of Av, 5750—Saddam gave Iraq's Revolution Command Council the green light to invade Kuwait. (This was revealed after the war in a BBC interview with then Iraqi Foreign Minister Tariq Aziz). At 2 A.M., August 2, an Iraqi force of 200,000 strong poured across the border into Kuwait and quickly overwhelmed the small military force defending the oil-rich Gulf state and its capital, Kuwait City.

Of course, anyone familiar with Jewish history knows how ominous the timing of these world-shaking events was. The "Three Weeks," culminating in *Tisha B'Av*, the ninth of Av, commemorate the siege and destruction of the first and second *Beis Hamikdash* (as well as other national tragedies). And although the destruction began on the ninth of Av, the fire raged, compelling our observance of some of the *halachos* (laws) of mourning into that date.

On this tenth day of Av, in the year 5750, the "Gulf War" was set in motion.

• The New D-Day

November 1990. The U.N. abandons diplomatic attempts to solve the crisis, and sets a deadline for withdrawal from Kuwait, authorizing the use of "all necessary means" to force Iraq to comply. A coalition of twenty-eight nations is formed, led by the U.S.A. and including Britain, France and several Arab nations. Over the next six months, the coalition builds up four times as many supplies as involved the invasion of Normandy on June 6, 1944, "D-Day." These include over 112,500 vehicles, 3,500 tanks, 2,000 armored vehicles, 1,000 helicopters and an average of 4,800 tons of supplies *per day*.

On January 17, 1991, U.S., British and Allied planes launch a massive campaign of missile strikes and aerial bombings. Saddam Hussein announces: "The mother of all battles is under way." Over the next six weeks, Allied planes fly more than 116,000 sorties, dropping an estimated total of 85,000 tons of bombs.

In response to the January 17 attack, Iraq fires SCUD missiles at civilian targets in Israel.

On February 24, 1991, Allied forces launch a combined ground, air and sea assault, which overwhelms the Iraqi army. During a 100-hour ground war, the 200,000 strong Iraqi army holding Kuwait is driven back.

On February 27, 1991, convoys of Allied troops enter Kuwait City to jubilant crowds. An estimated 25,000 to 30,000 Iraqis are killed during the ground war alone. Coalition forces across Iraq are capturing tens of thousands of Iraqi soldiers—hungry, exhausted and demoralized—surrendering with little resistance. (The U.S. estimated that 150,000 Iraqi soldiers had deserted.) Estimates of Iraqi deaths range from 60,000 to 200,000 soldiers. Heaps of Iraqi corpses litter the desert. The Coalition, on the other hand, loses 148 soldiers in battle (and another 145 in deaths described as "non-battle"). The next day, February 28, President George Bush, Sr. announces a ceasefire.

February 28, as all who lived through it remember, is Purim, the day commemorating the downfall of the scheming, thoroughly wicked Haman. A modern event that starts on the tenth of Av and ends on Purim—surely, it is an open message from heaven. Only a person completely unacquainted with Torah can fail to see the obvious hand of *Hashem* in the timing.

In any event, the Coalition pulls out, having accomplished the recapture of Kuwait and hoping that uprisings from dissidents in the north and south of Iraq will topple Saddam. No such overthrow occurs, however. Instead, a little over a year later, President Bush, Sr. is voted out of office while Saddam remains in power.

• Something Different: No Indifference

At the time, the spiritual lessons of the Gulf War seemed stunning enough. The first lesson—and hint that Someone Above is pulling strings behind the scenes—was that maybe the world had finally learned something from World War II. Saddam's designs depended on world indifference. How many weak countries had been overrun by stronger powers while the rest of the world stood by silently? As Tariq Aziz, in the BBC interview, said: "In 1975–1976, the Syrians invaded Lebanon. There was no reaction." Saddam had gassed the Kurdish people, and other than some ranting and raving, there was no world response.

He expected the same reaction with Kuwait. Indeed, Kuwait was to Saddam what the annexation of Czechoslovakia (the *Anschluss*) was to Hitler: a testing ground of the civilized world's mettle. If he could capture Kuwait, he would be that much closer to what many assumed was his next goal, Saudi Arabia—the country that sits on one quarter of the world's oil reserves. With Saddam in charge of such vast oil stores, he would in effect become the leader of an Arab Superstate. He would, indeed, become the modern day Nevuchadnezzar.

What the world failed to do about Hitler, however, it did in 1990. As President Bush said, they drew a line in the sand. They stood up to him, and not just with words.

Of course, a vital ingredient in the Coalition's ultimate success was another "little" piece of *hashgachah pratis*: seventy years of Soviet Communism was coming to an end. The Soviet Union, the main suppliers of Saddam's weaponry, was disintegrating. Had they been as strong as they had been during the height of the Cold War, the Middle East might have become the focal point of a new, incalculably more devastating, Superpower clash. However, when Saddam entered Kuwait, the Soviets were too preoccupied with their own problems. As a result, America imposed its will on world opinion to oppose Saddam.

The Gulf War

• The SCUDs

Yad Hashem.

The world was lined up against Saddam. A sizeable coalition had been put together, Arabs joining the Americans and Europeans. The only real threat to the coalition was Israel. The Arabs couldn't bear the thought of Jews killing Arabs. If the Israelis so much as fired one bullet, they would break off their support for the coalition.

As a result, countries such as Saudi Arabia, financier of the PLO, and Syria, the haven and training ground for terrorists, in essence told Israel, "Do not send one soldier. Do not fire one bullet. We will do your fighting for you."

Mind-boggling.

Just as mind-boggling, however, was the quandary this put Israel in. The modern secular state prided itself on the fact that it had eradicated the image of the weak ghetto Jew walking passively into a gas chamber. No, the modern Jew, the Israeli, would never let others kill him without going down with a fight. "Never again!" rang the battle cry. And, indeed, in four wars and countless battles, the Jewish soldier had proven a most formidable warrior, capable of miraculous victories despite seemingly overwhelming odds. Jews no longer needed others for protection. We will defend ourselves and not depend on anyone or anything. Not even *Hashem.* So rang the modern Israeli credo.

However, this situation challenged that ideology. The Israelis had to let whatever would happen happen and not respond, not join in the fray. The Coalition would destroy the SCUD launchers for them. They would protect Israel. This flew in the face of everything the secular founders of Israel stood for.

Saddam, an inveterate bully, sized up his situation. He saw how he was outnumbered. So what did he do? Did he fight his cause? No. Did he back down? No. He did something very much as Haman had done millennia before, as Hitler had done only decades earlier.

He blamed the Jews.

"Make the Israelis give the Palestinians autonomy, and Iraq will back out of Kuwait," he declared. "We are not aggressors bent on our own glory, but defenders of the Arab peoples against the real enemy, the Jews."

Then he threw down the gauntlet, threatening to level Tel Aviv with SCUD missiles if he was attacked. The Israelis would never stand for that, he thought gleefully. They would retaliate, and the Arabs would break off from the coalition!

President Bush refused to accept Saddam's attempt to transfer blame for the War over to the Israelis. "No linkage," Bush declared, meaning he would not listen to any discussion of a "link" between the demand that Saddam withdraw from Kuwait and the issue of Palestinian autonomy.

And Israel "sat on her hands," so to speak.

Of course, Saddam launched his SCUDs. Over the period of one month, thrity-nine SCUDs slammed Israel, primarily in metropolitan areas like Tel Aviv and Haifa. Miraculously, only one Israeli civilian[151] was killed by a direct hit (although several died from heart attacks and incorrect use of gas masks). In contrast, an Iraqi SCUD attack in February struck a building at the Dhahran U.S. base in Saudi Arabia and killed 28 U.S. military personnel.

• A Deeper Look

However, there is a poignant lesson in the SCUD attacks.

Thirty-nine SCUDs fell on Israel. "Thirty-nine" is a number Jews recognize. It is the number of *melachos*, "forms of labor," a Jew is forbidden to perform on *Shabbos*. On *Shabbos*, we refrain from action, and thereby acknowledge that we are not the power that runs the universe. There is a G-d. We are not the masters of our fate. *Hashem* is the Master. So, too, the major lesson of the Gulf War seems to be: *Hashem* runs the show. We don't.

Most of us will say that we know that lesson already; it's obvious. We'll say we believe it—after all, we say it in our prayers, in our *divrei*

The Gulf War

219

Torah (Torah discussions) and in various other ways numerous times a day. But do we really believe it? Do we live as though we believe it? This dichotomy is illuminated by a profound *Midrash*:

Four kings, David, Asa, Yehoshaphat and Chizkiyahu, each made a request to *Hashem*.

David said, "Let me chase my enemies and defeat them ...."

Asa said, "I have no strength to kill them, but I will chase them and You will do the rest ...."

Yehoshaphat said, "I have strength neither to kill nor to give chase. Rather I will praise the Almighty and You will do the rest ...."

Chizkiyahu said, "I have no strength to fight, chase or even praise the Almighty. Rather, I will sleep in bed, and You will do the rest ...." (*Yalkut Shmuel* 163).

According to the commentary *Anaf Yosef*, the four kings represent four *decreasing* levels of faith.[152] David and his generation were on such a high level of faith that when they pursued their enemies and defeated them, they still recognized that it was not their own might and power that had accomplished the deed. It was *Hashem*.

Asa and his generation were on a lower level. They could chase their enemies, but could not finish the deed. For if they did, they would have taken credit for themselves. So Asa asked *Hashem* to vanquish his enemies.

Yehoshaphat and his generation were even lower. All they could do was pray to *Hashem*. If they so much as chased their enemies, they would have thought they were the ones doing it. (And, indeed, the enemy armies besieging Yehoshaphat ended up slaughtering each other before they launched their attack.)

Chizkiyahu and his generation were even lower. Even after praying to *Hashem* for help, they would have accredited the victory to themselves. So all they could do was go to sleep. And sure enough, that night—*Pesach* night—the Assyrian army of 200,000 soldiers surrounding Jerusalem was wiped out by an Angel of *Hashem*.

It seems to me that this lowest level is similar to our experience in the Gulf War. Forced not to act, we were able to witness and acknowledge the miracles—such as SCUDs landing but not exploding—knowing we'd had no hand in them

Or perhaps we experienced a fifth level. We didn't even sleep. We got drunk and danced on Purim—*ad d'lo yada*—until we couldn't tell the difference between the curse of Haman and the blessing of Mordechai. When an evil tyrant like Saddam rises to power and is so ignobly defeated, it's a revelation of *yad Hashem*, the hand of G-d.

• Not With Armies

The theme of *yad Hashem* permeates the message of *Chanukah* as well, which Jews across the globe were preparing for as the news of Saddam's capture sank in. The special *haftarah* we read on *Shabbos Chanukah* summarized the essence not only of *Chanukah* but also of the Gulf War. After the prophet Zechariah is shown a vision of the *menorah* that will grace the future rebuilt *Beis Hamikdash*, he asks the angel who showed him the vision what it means. The angel answers him with one of the most famous lines in *Tanach*:

> "Not with armies, nor by power—but by My spirit, says the G-d [Commander-in-Chief] of [the Heavenly] Legions."
> (*Zechariah* 4:6)

Hashem is the Commander-in-Chief. Not Saddam. Not General Schwartzkopf. Not President Bush.

Moreover, the *menorah* in Zechariah's vision lit itself—each lamp "had seven ducts attached to the bowl on its top" (ibid., 4:3) from which oil flowed into the lamp *by itself*. *Chanukah*, and especially the *menorah*, drives home to us that regardless of our power, wealth, intelligence and greatest efforts, we do not run the show. A band of zealots can overthrow a superpower. A tiny cruse of oil meant to last one day can last for eight—if the Creator of heaven and earth so wills it.

Rabbi Moshe Weinberger of *Mesivta Beis Shraga* related how his father used to say that on Purim, the handle of the *gragger* (noisemaker) we spin is beneath the *gragger* itself, while on *Chanukah*, the handle of the *dreidel* (four-sided top) we spin is on top. Purim, he expounded, represents human initiative, an "awakening from below," while *Chanukah* represents Divine intervention, an "awakening from above." On Purim, we stir ourselves with drink, joy, a hearty meal and other activities. On *Chanukah*, we light a candle that we are not allowed to use for any purpose other than to gaze at its flame. We just sit back and look. We let *Hashem* take over. We remind ourselves that *Hashem* is running the show.

The Gulf War was essentially a modern reenactment of this theme.

• The Nevuchadnezzar Connection

It's no coincidence that Saddam fancied himself a reincarnated Nevuchadnezzar. Nevuchadnezzar teaches us one of the most important lessons in all *Tanach*:

> At the end of twelve months, he [Nevuchadnezzar] was walking atop the royal palace of Babylon. The king spoke, and said: "Isn't this Babylon, which I have built ... by the might of my power and for the glory of my *majesty*?" While the word was in the king's mouth ... at that moment ... Nevuchadnezzar [went mad and] ... was driven from the world of men, ate grass as oxen, his body was wet with the dew of heaven, his hair wild like an eagles' feathers, and his nails like birds' claws. (*Daniel* 4:26-28, 30)

A writer couldn't get away with writing this in a novel. It's too incredible to believe. Yet, the modern day Babylonian tyrant, who fashioned himself in the ancient tyrant's image, ends up on TV and in papers across the globe appearing just like Nevuchadnezzar as described in the book of *Daniel*, looking like a wild animal in a long beard and tangled hair. Truth is indeed stranger than fiction.

Of course, in *Tanach*, Nevuchadnezzar eventually regains his sanity and comes to this realization:

> And at the end of the days, I, Nevuchadnezzar, lifted up my eyes to heaven, and my understanding returned to me, and I blessed the Most High, and I praised and honored Him, the Eternal. For His dominion is an everlasting dominion, and His kingdom from generation to generation; and all the inhabitants of the earth are reputed as nothing; for He does according to His will in the host of heaven, and among the inhabitants of the earth. And none can stay His hand, or say unto Him: What are you doing .... Now I Nevuchadnezzar praise and extol and honor the King of heaven, for all His works are truth, and His ways justice; and those that walk in pride, He is able to abase. (*Daniel* 4:31-32, 34)

Nevuchadnezzar becomes the instrument of *kiddush Hashem* (sanctification of *Hashem's* name) like few others. He had conquered the world through great military, economic and "secular" might. He had reached the pinnacle, the apex. And there, at the zenith of his might, he fell—and fell as far as a human can fall, becoming something less than human.

Saddam, of course, did not become a world conqueror as Nevuchadnezzar, or the vehicle of *kiddush Hashem*—certainly not through his own volition. However, while the lesson did not penetrate his senses, it has ours, and hopefully, some of the rest of the world.

Hashem makes high and brings low. He turns kings into paupers and paupers into kings

"Not with armies, nor by power—but by My spirit, says the G-d [Commander-in-Chief] of [the Heavenly] Legions."

(Endnotes)

1   The Rambam writes: "... *Hashem* is aware of what is happening to us and He has the ability to correct our problems if we serve Him .... We should not believe that these occurrences are accidents or chance. This is the meaning of (*Vayikra* 26:21): *And if you walk with Me in the way of chance* ... In other words, I brought this suffering on you to correct you and if you think that it was merely chance [you will not look inwardly and] I will intensify this 'chance' to a harsh and unpleasant degree. This is the meaning of (*Vayikra* 26:27-28): *And if you walk with Me in the way of chance, then I will walk with you in the way of a furious chance.* That is because someone who believes all is chance will persist in his bad beliefs and corrupt deeds, and will not do *teshuva* ...." (*Moreh Nevuchim* 3:36; see also *Hilchos Taanis* 1:1-3)

2   Sometimes, rather than the generic term *hashgachah*, the term *hashgachah klalis* is used for events of a global nature, and *hashgachah pratis*, for events in our individual lives, down to the minutest detail.

3   From remarks by then President Ronald Reagan at the Annual National Prayer Breakfast, February 6, 1986.

4   There are two words most commonly used to mean faith: *emunah* (faith) and *bitachon* (trust). The Chazon Ish explains that *emunah* is theoretical, while *bitachon* is practical. *Bitachon* is the application of *emunah*. When a situation tests a person and he proceeds with the tranquil confidence that all is in the hands of Heaven, he is converting the raw potential of his *emunah* into *bitachon*.

5   Translation from *The Chazon Ish* (Mesorah Publications, Ltd., 1989), p. 150.

6   For example, the chapter on Pearl Harbor, "Day of Infamy," as well as the one on the *Titanic*, "A Titanic Lesson."

7   The Talmud (*Pesachim* 50a) teaches that one of the differences between the current world and the future world is that whereas now we have two blessings— thanking *Hashem* for the good (*hatov v'hamativ*) and acknowledging His justice for the bad (*dayan ha-emes*)—in the future, there will only be one: thanking *Hashem* for the good. I heard it explained this way: Now, for instance, if a person is saved from a ship that is sinking, he thanks *Hashem* for saving Him. In the future, though, a person will not only recognize and thank *Hashem* for saving him from the sinking ship, *but for being on the sinking ship in the first place!* We will achieve the perspective that all is for the good, even the times we were

put in peril and even the difficulties, challenges and downright scary, painful situations that caused us to need *Hashem's* saving Hands in the first place.

Nevertheless, now, and in general, while we live earthly lives, it is hard, if not virtually impossible, to achieve that divine perspective and understand how danger, suffering or death is good as we experience it. Rather than deny that, the Torah gives us the license to acknowledge our pain even as we intone a blessing that recognizes *Hashem* as the True Judge, who has a reason for everything He does or allows to happen.

8   *Am Olam: The History of the Eternal Nation; Vol. 1* (Feldheim), p. 15.

9   Note, of course, that there were certainly other battles of World War II, not to mention other wars of the twentieth century that could have been used toward the same end. Indeed, in the Holocaust book that the author is currently working on, the Nazi attacks on Soviet Russia (Barbarossa) and Stalingrad are analyzed for their *hashgachah* (in terms of both the elements of the general war as well as the war against the Jews).

10 Rambam, *Yesodei HaTorah* 1:1.

11 And this, according to Rabbi Samson Raphael Hirsch (*Commentary to the Torah*, Ex. 20:2), is implied by the very word *anochi*, "I," the way *Hashem* introduces Himself. There are different Hebrew words for "I." *Anochi* is the proclamation of intimate nearness between the speaker and the listener, Rabbi Hirsch writes. It is an "I" that encompasses "others" and is thereby infinitely more "whole."

12 The term "Maginot Line" has been used as a metaphor for something that is confidently relied upon, despite being ineffectual.

13 In August of 1938, Churchill visited the Maginot Line. His response is recorded in *Churchill: A Life*: "He was very impressed until he asked about the nature of the French defences from the point where the Maginot Line came to an end, to the coast at Dunkirk. When he was told the French only had some 'field works' guarding the two-hundred-mile gap, Churchill's face 'had ceased smiling,' Louis Spears, who accompanied him, later recalled, 'and the shake of his head was ominous when he observed that he hoped these field works were strong, that it would be very unwise to think the Ardennes were impassable to strong forces. 'Remember,' Churchill said, 'that we are faced with a new weapon, armour in great strength, on which the Germans are no doubt concentrating, and that forests will be particularly tempting to such forces since they will offer concealment from the air.' His words, of course, proved on this occasion as on so many others prophetic." (*Churchill: A Life*, p. 618)

14 Gamelin had set up his command post inside an enormous French palace described as a "submarine without a periscope." Almost unbelievably, it had no radio communications. It was not linked by teleprinter with any other headquarters in the field. Instead, messages were dispatched regularly on the hour by motorcycle.

15 From *Churchill: A Life*: "As the Dunkirk evacuation just began and things looked bleak, some in the British government considered surrender. Chamberlain said he would consider 'decent terms' if they were offered. Churchill was dismayed and angered. It was a thousand to one against any such 'decent terms' being offered, he explained. 'Nations which went down fighting rose again, but those who surrendered tamely were finished.' ... Churchill then revealed that as Prime Minister he had thought carefully for two days 'whether it was part of my duty to consider entering into negotiations with That Man.' The Germans would demand Britain's Fleet, her naval bases, and much else. Britain would become a 'slave state' with a puppet Government. Yet Britain still had 'immense reserves and advantages,' and, he concluded: 'If this long island story of ours is to end at last, let it end only when each one of us lies choking in his own blood upon the ground.'" (*Churchill: A Life*, p. 651)

16 *The Miracle of Dunkirk*, by Walter Lord, p. 25.

17 *The Miracle of Dunkirk*, p. 25.

18 Churchill replaced Neville Chamberlain on May 10, the day the Germans attacked. Chamberlain, the architect of appeasement and the policy of giving into Hitler's ever-growing demands in the hopes of a peace that would never come, was jeered by Parliamentary members mercilessly, the *coup de grace* being delivered by MP Leopold Amery. "Depart, I say," he shouted at Chamberlain, "and let us have done with you. In the name of G-d, go!" Following a vote of "no confidence," Chamberlain departed the building to chants of, "Go! Go! Go!"

19 "We were utterly speechless," [General] Heinz Guderian [architect of the attack] later declared, recalling the effect the halt order had on his tank commanders and crews .... General Colonel Walther von Brauchitsch, Chief of OKH—the Army's high command—wondered about the same thing ... It seemed an incredible step. And even more incredible to take it without consulting the Army's top command. Summoned to Hitler's headquarters that evening, he was prepared to argue his case. He never had a chance. He got a chewing out instead .... Ranting at the unfortunate General, he ... reconfirmed the halt order. At 8:20 P.M., Brauchitsch returned to OKH angry and humiliated. His Chief of Staff General Franz Halder was in an even worse mood .... On the morning of May 25, the two Generals went back to the

Führer for one more try. Prolonging the halt order, Brauchitsch argued, meant nothing less than risking certain victory. As the campaign had been planned, Army Group A was the hammer and B the anvil; now the hammer was being stopped in midair ... Hitler would have none of it." (*The Miracle of Dunkirk*, pp. 30-31)

20 "From a mobile headquarters train, hidden in a forest near the Franco-German border, General Field Marshal Hermann Goering also followed the dash of the panzers with mounting concern. But his worries had little to do with exposed flanks or mechanical breakdowns. Goering, an exceptionally vainglorious man, was Commander-in-Chief of the Luftwaffe, and he was worried that these dramatic tactics were robbing his air force of its proper share in the coming victory .... A call was immediately put through to Hitler at his forest headquarters, near the village of Miinstereifel in northwestern Germany. Goering poured out his case: This was the moment to turn the Luftwaffe loose. If the Führer would order the army to stand back and give him room, he guaranteed his planes would wipe out the enemy. It would be a cheap victory, and the credit would go to the air arm, associated with the new Reich of National Socialism, rather than to the army generals and old-line Prussian aristocrats." (*The Miracle of Dunkirk*, p. 28)

21 On June 4, after the evacuation was completed, Churchill delivered one of his most famous and inspiring speeches: "We shall go on to the end. We shall fight in France, we shall fight on the seas and oceans," he proclaimed in defiance. "... We shall fight on the beaches, we shall fight on the landing grounds, we shall fight in the fields and in the streets, we shall fight in the hills; we shall never surrender." (*Churchill: A Life*, p. 657)

Despite the success of *Operation Dynamo*, the Dunkirk operation, over 50,000 vehicles and 40,000 French troops were abandoned after a valiant effort to save them. The British also lost 235 ships of various types.

22 In his speech to Parliament on June 4. A couple of weeks earlier, when things were looking particularly grim, Churchill remarked to Anthony Eden, "About time No. 17 turned up, isn't it?" The reference was to a game of roulette he had once won by playing #17.

23 The *Av Harachamim* prayer, recited on *Shabbos* after the Torah reading, was written in response to the Crusades. In it, we memorialize the righteous martyrs and pray for retribution for their spilled blood. Although not generally recited on *Shabbos* days that have an added celebratory nature—such as *Shabbos Mevarchim*—in many congregations it's recited during *Sefiras HaOmer* even when we bless the new months of Iyar and Sivan. The *Mishnah Berurah* (284:18) adds that even if there is a *bris milah* (circumcision) that *Shabbos*,

giving us a second reason why *Av Harachamim* should not be recited, it is nevertheless still said, since this was the season of the tragedies.

24 Perhaps this is one reason why, after we count the *omer* each of the 49 nights between *Pesach* and *Shavuos*, we conclude our counting with the words, "*HaRachaman*—Merciful One—restore to the *Beis Hamikdash* ...."

25 Another advantage the British had that would prove pivotal was that RAF pilots who bailed out of their aircraft could be back at their airfields within hours. Luftwaffe aircrews, on the other hand, either were captured or drowned in the English Channel.

26 Despite the devastation in England, British aircraft were being replaced faster than those of the Germans. "Aircraft factories in England, one of the prime targets of the Luftwaffe bombers, actually out-produced the Germans in 1940 by 9,924 to 8,070 planes." (*Rise and Fall*, p. 781) The problem was replacing pilots. Luckily, the RAF, reluctantly at first, incorporated pilots from other nationalities, including Australians, South Africans, New Zealanders and Canadians as well as Czech and Polish squadrons. Free French, Belgian and some American pilots also joined the RAF.

27 The Air Marshall's exact quote, confirmed a translator at the Nuremberg trial who heard it from Goering directly, was: "If Allied planes ever bomb Berlin, you can call me Meyer."

28 "The RAF came over in greater force on the night of August 28-29 and for the first time killed Germans in the capital of the Reich. The official count was ten killed and twenty-nine wounded. The Nazi bigwigs were outraged. Goebbels, who had ordered the press to publish only a few lines on the first attack, now gave instructions to cry out at the "brutality" of the British flyers in attacking the defenceless women and children of Berlin. Most of the capital's dailies carried the same headline: COWARDLY BRITISH ATTACK. Two nights later, after the third raid, the headlines read: BRITISH AIR PIRATES OVER BERLIN!" (*Rise and Fall of the Third Reich*, by William Shirer, p. 778)

29 "Some 842 people were killed and 2,347 wounded ... during these first two nights, and vast damage was inflicted on the sprawling city ...." (*Rise and Fall of the Third Reich*, p. 780)

30 More than 23,000 British civilians lost their lives during the raids of 1940 and over 32,000 were wounded. One of the largest single raids occurred on December 29, 1940, in which almost 3,000 civilians died.

31 Winston Churchill coined the name of the battle in a speech to the House of Commons after the defeat of France: "What General Weygand called the Battle of France is over. I expect that the *Battle of Britain* is about to begin."

Historians divide the Battle of Britain into four phases: 1) July 10–August 11: *Kanalkampf*, Luftwaffe targets shipping in the English Channel. 2) August 12–August 23: *Adlerangriff*, assault against the coastal airfields. 3) August 24–September 6: The critical phase of the battle. 4) September 7 onwards: attacks switch to London.

32 Post-war analysis of records has shown that between July and September the RAF lost 1,023 fighter aircraft, while the Luftwaffe losses stood at 1,887, of which 873 were fighters. "Hitler's bomber losses over England had been so severe that they could never be made up, and in fact the Luftwaffe, as the German confidential records make clear, never fully recovered from the blow it received in the skies over Britain that late summer and fall." (*Rise and Fall of the Third Reich*, p. 781)

33 September 15 is celebrated in Britain as "Battle of Britain Day," marking the climactic battles above London. However, after September 15, a scaled down German air offensive continued until the beginning of the German invasion of Russia in June 1941.

34 The victory was as much psychological as physical. It turned a tide of defeats and heartened the enemies of Nazism. The British victory marked the first failure of Hitler's war machine. It also signalled a shift in American opinion at a time when many Americans believed that Britain could not survive.

35 Cited in *The Call of the Torah*, by Rabbi Elie Munk.

36 The Nazi pilot who lost his way, leading to his nation's eventual defeat, is even more conspicuous when compared to the American pilot, just a few months later, who lost his way but thereby discovered the hidden Japanese fleet and thus ensured victory for the Americans in the pivotal Battle of Midway; see next chapter.

37 From the Talmud (*Pesachim* 50a): The Rabbis commented on the verse: *On that day Hashem will be One and His Name One* (*Zechariah* 14:9). "Is not He One now, too?" Rabbi Acha bar Chanina said, "The World-to-Come is not like this world. In this world, one pronounces the blessing 'Who is good and bestows good' upon hearing good news, and the blessing 'the true Judge,' upon hearing bad news, whereas in the World-to-Come there will be only one blessing: 'Who is good and does good.'"

Similarly, the Talmud (*Berachos* 60b) states that Rabbi Akiva said a person should always accustom himself to say: "Everything the Merciful one does is for the good."

38 Rabbi Nachman of Breslov articulated this particularly well: "Indeed, there is no evil in the world, only complete goodness. The suffering that comes from all the afflictions that beset us results from the lack of knowledge that makes us unable to consider the ultimate purpose, which is all good, and hence we feel the pain and the hurt. But when we have knowledge and consider the ultimate purpose, we feel no pain or suffering ...." (*Likutei Moharan* I: 65:3)

39 Historian John Toland's book, *Infamy*, caused a stir when it was first published in 1982. *Infamy* puts together evidence strongly suggesting that Franklin Roosevelt and others were aware of the Pearl Harbor attack before it happened and not only did nothing to prevent it but intentionally ignored it. Why would FDR and/or other higher-ups know about such an attack and not tell anyone? Simply put, they wanted a reason to bring the previously ambivalent nation into the war. And, in fact, the uproar in the U.S. in the aftermath of the attack enraged the nation and drove it into the Pacific War with abandon. Shouts of "Remember Pearl Harbor" became the battle cry for tens of millions of Americans. Of course, that alone doesn't prove it. The facts are, however, that by late 1941 it was more than apparent that war was coming with Japan. The Americans had broken the Japanese code and were intercepting all messages sent by Tokyo to its embassy in Washington. Whether or not the attack was invited, or specific warnings were ignored (as Toland puts forth), the bottom line is that he offers no absolute proof that FDR and/or the State and War Departments knew that Pearl Harbor was about to be hit. He does, however, offer some impressive circumstantial evidence. After all is said and done, the jury is still out on the verdict.

40 The bombers were supposed to be launched from the carrier Hornet some 450 to 650 miles from Japan. However, an enemy patrol boat had been spotted and the Americans worried their presence had been discovered. They therefore launched the planes immediately, about 800 miles from Japan. All of the B-25s reached the Japanese islands, dropped their bombs on oil stores, factory areas, and military installations and then headed out across the East China Sea because they had no fuel to return to their carrier. Doolittle and sixty-two other U.S. airmen parachuted to safety with friendly Chinese, four drowned and one was killed baling out. The Japanese captured eight airmen and executed three of them for "inhuman acts." Another died in a prison camp, but seventy-one of the eighty heroic fliers survived the war.

41 The Battle of the Coral Sea took place May 4-8, 1942. It marked the first time in history that naval fleets engaged in a duel completely out of sight of each other, through airplanes originating from enemy aircraft carriers. Even though the Americans lost the aircraft carrier *Lexington* (two Japanese carriers were damaged and unavailable for Midway) the Battle of the Coral Sea was a standoff. After five months of continuous defeat, though, the standoff was a moral victory for the Americans. At the very least, it proved to them that the Japanese were not completely invincible.

42 Even years before Pearl Harbor, Japanese pilots had undergone the most intensive training program and gained real-time experience in their one-sided war with China.

43 By contrast, the two Japanese carriers that were damaged at the Coral Sea— the *Zuikaku* and *Shokaku*—took as much as six months to repair. If either carrier had been able to take part in the crucial battle of Midway, the results might have been different.

44 Ensign George H. Gay (1917-1994) managed to get out of his torpedoed plane after it crashed into the sea and before it sank. Hiding himself under a rubber seat cushion to avoid strafing (the Japanese would shoot helpless survivors in the water to prevent them from rescue and flying again), he had a front row seat to the greatest sea-battle in history. Gay was picked up by an American seaplane the next day and became an instant celebrity when his story was reported in the papers.

45 After the Japanese carriers of Nagumo's First Air Fleet were destroyed, they still had a lethal naval force of aircraft carriers, battleships and other vessels sailing a day behind, led by their Supreme Commander Admiral Yamamoto. In fact, with seven battleships, this second group was considered the main battle fleet. They were designed to finish off the U.S. fleet after the carriers of Nagumo's fleet inflicted their damage. And the Americans still had no idea they were in the vicinity. Yamamoto hoped, even after the disastrous defeat of his initial striking force, to draw the American carriers into an ambush and destroy them with his still formidable power. However, another stroke of luck saved the Americans. The best, most aggressive admiral, Bill "Bull" Halsey, had contracted a mysterious skin disease just before the battle and was in a Pearl Harbor hospital recovering during the entire battle. Serving in his place was Admiral Raymond Spruance, an inexperienced but highly capable temporary replacement. However, whereas Halsey was known, even to the Japanese, for his extreme aggressiveness, Spruance was relatively conservative. The Japanese did not know Halsey was hospitalized and had not taken part in the battle. They therefore expected the American fleet to pursue the surviving ships of

Nagumo's task force, thereby sailing straight into an ambush that could easily have led to disaster, including the sinking of the two remaining aircraft carriers. However, fate (i.e., *yad Hashem*) had intervened when it struck Halsey with his mysterious, short-lived skin ailment, because "Bull" probably would have continued the attack. Admiral Spruance, however, was satisfied with his victory and did not want to risk his carriers to pursue remnants of Nagumo's fleet. After about a day of waiting, when Yamamoto saw the American's were not going to fall into his ambush, he withdrew his force, never realizing that it was a simple skin ailment that saved the Americans!

46   The U.S. lost 307 men, one carrier (the *Yorktown*), one destroyer and 147 aircraft. The Japanese lost 2,500 men, 4 carriers, one heavy cruiser, and 332 aircraft. American industrial power was able to replace American losses much quicker than the Japanese. At least as significant, the Japanese couldn't replace their top, combat-tested pilots. (The Americans would promote experienced pilots to educational roles, which enabled them to pass on their know-how and experience. The Japanese, by contrast, had no such system; when an experienced Japanese pilot was lost, so was his experience.)

47   When American sea-planes spotted the Japanese fleet at around 7 A.M. on June 4, Admiral Spruance, in command of the American fleet, had a decision to make. If he launched his planes immediately, he might catch the Japanese at their most vulnerable. However, he was approximately two hours away from the ideal launch point, which would have allowed his planes to strike and return. If he launched immediately, they would not have enough fuel to return. Nevertheless, that's what he decided to do: launch immediately. Yet, for reasons that have never been clear, Spruance's intentions were not clearly communicated to *Hornet*—the second carrier in the fleet—and *Hornet* did not know of the launch until seven minutes before the scheduled time! There were also inexcusable delays once the planes were up in the air. Some circled for almost an hour waiting for squadrons to form up, while others unwittingly left early due to miscommunication. On top of all this, planes from the third U.S. carrier, *Yorktown*, were held in reserve and did not launch until close to 9 A.M. that morning. Afterwards, it was admitted that this was a mistake, since in carrier warfare the idea was to get as many planes up in the air to sink the enemy's carriers before they could sink yours.

48   Another intervention of *yad Hashem* was the strange, sudden illness that came upon air operations officer, Minoru Genda. Admiral Nagumo was an old-school naval officer, and had little feel for naval air warfare. He relied heavily upon Genda, a brilliant officer who had worked out the plans for the attack on Pearl Harbor. Just before the battle, however, Genda became ill, and did not even leave with the attackers. Some speculate that had Genda been well and

available, he would not have allowed Nagumo to make the mistakes that led to the destruction of the First Air Fleet.

49   The expression "D-Day" has come to mean the greatest single Allied operation of World War II, the invasion of Normandy. However, originally, before becoming associated with the Normandy invasion, "D-Day" was exclusively a military term referring to the first day ("D" for "day") of any military operation during the war. The second day was D+2, the third day, D+3, etc.

50   Had they been merged together nine planes wide, the aerial train ferrying the three Allied airborne divisions to Normandy on June 5 would have extended two hundred miles in length (*Eisenhower*, p. 528). Besides the naval bombardment, 5,000 tons of bombs would hit the German defenses from the air. Many planes, however, were used to transport supplies and parachute troops behind enemy lines.

51   The Allied invasion plans included a massive, sophisticated "Deception Plan" called "Operation Fortitude" to fool the Germans into believing the invasion would come from the north at Calais, the Nazi-controlled French port closest the English coast. They created a fictitious army and called it the "First U.S. Army Group." They concocted fake buildings and equipment and sent false radio messages. They even assigned their greatest general, George Patton, as its commander.

The invasion preparations also included some highly unusual armored vehicles known as "Hobart's Funnies," named for General Percy Hobart, who designed them. Among "Hobart's Funnies" was a mine-clearing tank (the "Sherman Crab," which was a normal Sherman tank fitted with flailing chains to its front, designed to destroy mines without damaging the tank), a "swimming tank," a bridge-laying tank and a road-laying tank. Most ingenious of all (although not Hobart's) were the "Mulberry Harbors," two huge barges filled with 600,000 tons of cement, creating 10 miles of floating roadways, which were towed across the English Channel to create a breakwater that would allow ships to land supplies and troops on the beaches of Normandy. Although towed across the Channel on June 9, a vicious storm destroyed one of the Mulberry Harbors on June 19. The other one, referred to as "Port Winston" (since English Prime Minister Winston Churchill authorized it), helped land over 2.5 million men, 500,000 vehicles and 4 million tons of supplies in the 100 days following D-Day.

52   Although ultimately successful, D-Day was only the beginning of the Battle of Normandy, which lasted until August 1944. Over 400,000 Allied and German troops were killed, wounded or went missing during the Battle of Normandy. This figure includes over 200,000 Allied casualties, including 54,000 dead.

Roughly 200,000 German troops were killed or wounded. During the fighting around the Falaise Pocket (August 1944) alone, the Germans suffered losses of around 90,000, including prisoners.

53 "The morning of June 6, Adolf Hitler was asleep at the Berghof, his Bavarian retreat in Berchtesgaden, unaware of what was transpiring in Normandy. As each fresh report from Army Group B and OB West brought increasingly unfavorable news, no one dared wake the habitually late-rising Hitler until nearly noon. The time lost by failing to wake the Führer was critical. When he learned of the airborne landings, [General] von Rundstedt immediately ordered two veteran panzer divisions to be held in reserve (Panzer Lehr and the 12th SS) to the Caen sector [in Normandy], but because OKW [Hitler's headquarters] retained control over their employment, von Rundstedt elected to request formal permission. Fearful of Hitler's wrath, OKW refused, and the only two formations that might have made a difference on June 6, sat uselessly until 4:00 P.M. that afternoon, when Hitler ordered their commitment. It was too little, too late. How much of a difference they could have made is open to debate, however. Only if they had moved at night would either division have escaped decimation by Allied aircraft." (*Eisenhower*, pp. 530-531)

54 "On this day, June 5, he [Eisenhower] drank one pot of coffee after another and was once heard to mutter, 'I hope to G-d I know what I'm doing.'" (*Eisenhower: A Soldier's Life*, by Carlo D'Este, Henry Holt and Company, 2002, p. 1)

55 On June 5, 1944, Eisenhower scribbled what historians call his "In Case Of Failure" message: "Our landings in the Cherbourg-Havre area have failed to gain a satisfactory foothold and I have withdrawn the troops. My decision to attack at this time and place was based upon the best information available. The troops, the air and the Navy did all that bravery and devotion to duty could do. If any blame or fault attaches to the attempt it is mine alone." Luckily, Eisenhower never had to use it, but the fact that he had written it shows just as precarious his decision was to go ahead.

56 "At the late-evening briefing [on June 5, 1944], Eisenhower presided over one of the most important councils of war in military history. The sounds of rain and the wind howling in rage outside could distinctly be heard by the assembled generals, admirals, and air marshals. Eisenhower's trademark smile was missing, replaced by an air of solemnity .... This was possibly the most important weather prediction in history: A mistaken forecast for D-Day could turn the entire tide of the war in Europe against the Allies. His [Eisenhower's] heart and his head told him that he must trust Stagg [the Allies' chief meteorologist] and his weather forecast. The invasion must go ahead. It was a very slender thread on which to base the fate of the war, but it was all

Eisenhower had. 'I am quite positive we must give the order,' he said. 'I don't like it but there it is .... I don't see how we can do anything else.' With that low-key pronouncement, the invasion of Normandy would take place the morning of June 6, based on the most important weather forecast in history ....' (*Eisenhower*, pp. 522-524)

57 Of course, the idea of a "new century" was artificial. The nice, round year "1900" of the Common Era, for instance, was in actuality the less-than-perfectly-round year 5560 on the Jewish calendar. Even the year 1900 of the "Common Era" calendar was a misnomer. Historians in the late nineteenth century, using sparse historical records from ancient Rome, Greece, Mesopotamia and Egypt, worked backward to arrive at the assumed birth date of Christianity's founder. Many scholars today disagree with this dating and move the date back to between 4 and 30 BCE.

58 "The Enlightenment" was a current of ideas and attitudes in thought and culture that appeared in Europe, first in France, in the late seventeenth and eighteenth centuries. Originating in France, it spread to England and Germany—climaxing with the American and French Revolutions. The Declaration of Independence is a reflection of Enlightenment ideology; for example, its statement that people were given natural inalienable rights by the Creator and created equal. Many Enlightenment thinkers also believed in the *absolute* power of human reason to correct all evils. While this may have been helpful in breaking the power of the medieval Church, excessive faith in the power of human reason—denying the higher-than-reason Revelation at Sinai—can create its own moral dilemmas, including these exhortations: "Lest ... your heart become haughty, and you will forget *Hashem* your G-d." (*Devarim* 8:12, 14) and "My strength and the might of my arm produced all this wealth for me" (*Devarim* 8:17).

59 Barbara Tuchman, *Guns Of August*, p. 440.

60 *Ibid.*, p. 440.

61 In 1894, Captain Alfred Dreyfus of the French army was falsely accused of treason and sentenced to life imprisonment. A public controversy that brought out the worst in many Frenchmen, the Dreyfus Affair demonstrated to assimilated Jews that old hatreds and suspicions of Jews were still alive in the public imagination and could be easily brought to the surface. It also demonstrated that no matter how assimilated and patriotic Jews were—Dreyfus was a model "Frenchman"—their non-Jewish neighbors, deep down, viewed them as different.

62   On the first day of Easter, April 6, 1903, several hundred Christians, incited by a blood libel spread by a local government-subsidized newspaper, began a pogrom in the Russian town of Kishinev. They broke windows and robbed small shops, while police stood by and watched. The inaction of the authorities convinced them that the Czar himself had given the permission to beat and raid the Jews, and was the catalyst to the next day's mayhem. Indeed, a garrison of 5,000 soldiers stationed in the city, which could easily have held back the mob, took no action. Here is an excerpt of a description of the pogrom printed in the *New York Times*: "It is impossible to account the amounts of goods destroyed in a few hours. The hurrahs of the rioting, and the pitiful cries of the victims filled the air. Wherever a Jew was met, he was savagely beaten into insensibility. One Jew was dragged from a streetcar and beaten until the mob thought he was dead. The air was filled with feathers and torn bedding. Every Jewish household was broken into and the unfortunate Jews in their terror endeavored to hide in cellars and under roofs. The mob entered the synagogue, desecrated the biggest house of worship, and defiled the Scrolls of the Law. The conduct of the intelligent Christians was disgraceful. They made no attempt to check the rioting. They simply walked around enjoying the frightful sport. On Tuesday, the third day, when it became known that the troops had received orders to shoot, the rioters ceased." In the end, official records show that 49 Jews had been killed, 587 injured, 1,350 houses and 588 shops destroyed during the pogrom. Under the pressure of public opinion, some of the perpetrators of the pogrom were brought to justice. However, they were awarded very lenient sentences.

63   *World of Our Fathers*, p. 126.

64   The Hebrew date was the ninth of Av, *Tisha B'Av*, the most tragic day on the Jewish calendar, commemorating the destruction of both the First and Second Temple.

65   "*What is this that we have done?*" (*Shemos* 14:5) The *Midrash* explains the Egyptians' consternation upon realizing that by freeing the Jews they lost their dominance over the world. The *Midrash* concludes with the interesting observation that those nations who enslaved the Jews were always at that time foremost among world powers. However, as soon as they banished the Jews from their land, they lost their pre-eminence. (*The Call of the Torah*, p. 168)

66   A firsthand account from an immigrant about the ordeal of crossing the Atlantic: "On board the ship, we became utterly dejected. We were all herded together in a dark, filthy compartment in the steerage. … Wooden bunks had been put up in two tiers. … Seasickness broke out among us. Hundreds of people had vomiting fits, throwing up even their mother's milk. … As all were

crossing the ocean for the first time, they thought their end had come. The confusion of cries became unbearable. ... I wanted to escape from that inferno, but no sooner had I thrust my head forward from the lower bunk than someone above me vomited straight upon my head. I wiped the vomit away, dragged myself onto the deck, leaned against the railing and vomited my share into the sea, and lay down half—dead upon the deck." (*World Of Our Fathers*, pp. 40-41)

Among the other deprivations of the cross-Atlantic voyage was food. There wasn't much to eat: rolls that were either hard as rocks or soggy with salt water. Sometimes, the passengers were "treated" to watery soup, which was more like a mud puddle than soup. Jews who kept kosher often didn't even have that. They rationed a small amount of stale bread and drank boiled water that, if they were lucky, might be mixed with a little brandy and sugar to give it a taste.

They slept where they ate, in hard, cramped bunks, usually three tiers high, freezing when the hatch was open, and suffocating from the pungent stench of unwashed bodies, spoiled food and vomit when it was closed. The only light came from a dim, swaying lantern. Night and day were often indistinguishable.

Toilets and washrooms were primitive. Cold salt water was the only thing available for washing, and keeping clean was nearly impossible. Even in calm seas, people felt continually seasick. When a real storm broke out, the ship heaved so much that people vomited all over the place, even on top of each other. You could hear the crashing of dishes and the shrieking of scared children, thinking their end had come. They were ever aware of the treacherous winds and waves, the scampering of rats and the splash of sea burials. One in ten failed to survive the crossing.

67 For the millions of steerage-class immigrants who came to America, the joy of seeing the Statue for the first time was often followed by the traumatic experience of Ellis Island. (In truth, immigrants arrived in many American ports, but the port of New York, and its reception area at Ellis Island, was the most famous and traversed. An estimated 40% of Americans can trace their ancestry back to someone who passed through Ellis Island.) After the ship anchored, the passengers disembarked onto a barge that took them to the dock. From there they formed a line, three abreast, that stretched into the Main Building and up a winding staircase to the second floor. As they climbed the steep stairs, doctors at the top watched them closely. In no more than a few seconds, they checked the new arrivals for symptoms of disease, disability or any number of conditions. If a person was breathing heavily from the climb, the doctor would put an "H" in chalk mark on the immigrant's clothing, meaning possible heart problem. If his eyes were wild and confused, the doctor

would mark an "X," indicating suspected mental illness. On average, one immigrant in every five required further medical examination. Eventually, all the immigrants were led into the Registry Room, a great hall serving as a veritable "Tower of Babel," filled with the sounds of languages from the four corners of the Earth. Jews in long beards, Italians with curled moustaches, Cossacks carrying swords, Arabs in long robes—all mingled together in a colorful throng. At the far end of the Registry Hall, inspectors in starched collars stood behind tall desks. Interpreters fluent in major languages and obscure dialects assisted the inspectors, verifying information already contained on the manifest sheet. Although the actual interrogation lasted only a matter of minutes, the inspection process took an average of five hours to complete.

68   In actuality, the plaque remained nothing more than an obscure footnote for an entire generation. However, with the dark storm clouds of World War II gathering in the 1930s, and waves of dislocated immigrants from fascist countries clanging at the doors of America, the poem became part of the public's consciousness, quoted again and again in speeches, and immortalized in the music like that of famous songwriter Irving Berlin. For the first time, the key lines were widely acknowledged to represent the quintessential idea of America.

69   The French had built the Statue of Liberty in 1886 as a gift to the U.S., calling it "Liberty Enlightening the World." Emma Lazarus, however, in her famous poem, "The New Colossus," called the statue, "Mother of Exiles." This was a reference to *Rachel Imainu*, "Mother Rachel," whose tomb in *Eretz Yisrael* marks the spot 2,500 years ago where masses of Jews, just defeated by the Babylonian army, were led into exile. At their most desperate hour, the sight of the tomb of their Mother Rachel gave them comfort, for the *navi* had said:

"... A voice of lament can be heard in Ramah, and bitter weeping; Rachel weeps for her children, refusing to be comforted for her children, because they were not." (*Yirmiyahu* 31:14)

To Emma Lazarus, the parallel between the Jews who suffered exile in ancient Babylon and modern Czarist Russia was unmistakable.

70   The Pale, originally created in 1791 by Catherine the Great, and redefined in 1835 by Czar Alexander I, was actually a compromise between those elements in the Russian government who espoused complete expulsion of the Jews, and those more serious about Enlightenment ideas. Russian society was traditionally feudal, divided sharply between the nobles (the "haves") and serfs (the "have nots"). Enlightenment ideas seeped into feudal Russia slowly, but eventually led to the emergence of a middle class, which was rapidly filled by

Jews. By limiting their area of residence, the powers-that-be were ensuring the growth of a Russian middle class. One result of this policy was that it forced Jews to move to small provincial towns, fostering the rise of the *shtetls* (literally, "little cities," from the German, *stadt*).

Czar Alexander III's goal for returning Jews to the Pale was more nefarious, as explained ahead.

71 The plaque of the famous poem about the Statue of Liberty was put up on May 5, 1903, which coincides with 8 Iyar, the 23rd day of the *omer*—the days between *Pesach* and *Shavuos*. It's almost as if the message is that America represents liberty, but falls short of freedom.

72 Perhaps this is why we say in *Dayenu* that it would have been enough had *Hashem* taken us out of Egypt but not brought us to Sinai to receive the Torah. How can that be? The truth is, though, that the exhilaration of liberty, even just "freedom from," is something to thank *Hashem* for endlessly. Liberty is something never to be taken for granted. One can't truly appreciate liberty until one loses it.

73 *Michtav MeiEliyahu* II, "*U'geulah Ha'asidah*," pp. 19-21.

74 Analyses of the 1990 *National Jewish Population Survey* (NJPS) data by Sylvia Barak Fishman and Alice Goldstein (1993) report that Jewish adults with six or more years of day school Jewish education are more likely than those with minimal or no Jewish education to marry another Jew. Moreover, in their examination of the 1990 NJPS data, Mordechai Rimor and Elihu Katz (1993) concluded that the Jewish Day School was "... the only schooling that stands against the assimilatory process indicated by intermarriage and its related behaviors." Although Rimor and Katz agree with Fishman and Goldstein in principle, they maintain that nine or more years of Jewish education are necessary to make a strong impact on adult Jewish behavior. See further, the analysis of the 1990 NJPS by Antony Gordon and Richard Horowitz at Aish. com, "Will Your Grandchildren be Jews?" (http://www.aish.com/jewishissues/ jewishsociety/Will_Your_Grandchildren_Be_Jews$.asp); also see *The Vanishing American Jew* by Alan M. Dershowitz (Little Brown & Co., 1997), p. 26.

75 See *Reb Shraga* (Mesorah Publications, Ltd.) by Yonasan Rosenblum for a biography of his life.

76 A Model-T cost about $300 in the late 1920s. The *weekly* salary of the average worker was about $17-$22 in 1929.

77 Farmers were especially hard-hit by the Great Depression. Many had gone into debt to buy machinery and land, and now could not make their payments. Low

crop prices wiped out potential profits. In addition to the usual problems, a great drought took place in 1931-32 in the Midwest and the South, turning much of the trans-Mississippi West into what became known as the "dust bowl."

78 *Zohar, Vayikra* 31b.

79 McGovern was one of the pilots who had bombed the I.G. Farben rubber factory in August, 1944, that used slave labor from Auschwitz-Birkenau. Although the factory was a mere five miles from the crematoria, and Allied bomber pilots had Auschwitz within their gun sights, they were never given the order to attack. Later research confirmed that had the pilots been told to bomb the crematoria they could have done so with relative ease, without compromising the general war effort, despite claims to the contrary by the Allied war department leaders at the time. Years later, McGovern said about this: "Franklin Roosevelt was a great man and he was my political hero. But I think he made two great mistakes in World War Two. One was the internment of Japanese-Americans; the other was the decision not to go after Auschwitz ... G-d forgive us for that tragic miscalculation."

80 He actually noticed it twice. The first time, he took it off and didn't report anything. However, the intruders came down, saw the tape was removed and put it back on! When the guard saw it the second time, that's when he called the police.

81 The next day, after attaining search warrants, police found more burglary tools and electronic bugging equipment stashed in six suitcases, plus "another $4,200 in $100 bills of the same serial number sequence as the money taken from the suspects."

82 For example, a fake letter written on Senator Edmund Muskie's letterhead called French-Canadians, "Canucks," a derogatory name. The letter was published as authentic. Muskie denied it, but the damage was done, and it led to his defeat in the Democratic primary. Woodward and Bernstein later discovered that the letter was forged by the Deputy Director of Communications at the White House, Ken Clawson. The White House had him forge the letter, fearing that Muskie, a moderate, would prove a more challenging opponent to Nixon than McGovern, whose liberalism was more extreme.

83 *All the President's Men,* pp. 134-5.

84 Kissinger was born in Germany to a Jewish family who fled the Nazis in 1938, settling in New York. He played a dominant role in foreign affairs during Nixon's terms and beyond, winning the Nobel Peace Prize for his efforts in

Vietnam. He remains, nevertheless, a controversial figure among both anti-war liberals and anti-Communist hawks for his foreign policy decisions.

85 What goes around comes around (*midah k'neged midah*, in Torah terms)—his attempt to bug others led to his downfall when he bugged himself.

86 Other Arab countries, including Saudi Arabia, Kuwait and Libya, supplied financial aid. Iraq sent 18,000 Iraqi soldiers and a few 100 tanks. Libya, Algeria, Tunisia and Morocco sent [combined] a few thousand soldiers, as well as some tanks, fighters and bombers.

87 Nixon related this himself in the film documentary, "A Nation Is Born."

88 Note: Nothing in this chapter is meant to pass judgment on the moral worth or lack thereof of "Deep Throat's" decision to inform on Nixon. The purpose of this article, rather, has only been to show one piece of possible *hashgachah* in *Hashem's* manipulation of events; how even a seemingly unrelated action, in a parking garage thousands of miles away taking place more than a year earlier, can become part of the Master Designer's plan for *Klal Yisrael*.

89 "The Wall Cracks: November 9, 1989," by Michael Meyer, Daniel Pedersen and Karen Breslau for *Newsweek*, November 20, 1989.

90 *Loc. cit.*

91 *Loc. cit.*

92 Nevertheless, the Allies continued airlifting supplies into Berlin until September 1949, in case the Soviet withdrawal was a ruse.

93 Thus, the American policy toward Communist expansion became known as "Containment." Historically, it began with the Truman Doctrine, which declared that the United States would support "free peoples who are resisting attempted subjugation by armed minorities or by outside pressures." The doctrine was specifically aimed at assisting governments resisting communism.

94 The Cold War also had a profound effect on how the U.S. and her allies treated the Germans. All the Allied powers, including the Americans who entered the fray against Hitler relatively late, had a deep hatred for anything and everything Nazi. After destroying the German army, they indicted, jailed and executed many Nazis, trying most of the worst criminals in the city of Nuremberg—the very place where the Nazis had held their most grandiose rallies and hypnotically converted the masses to their ideological beliefs. The Allies waged an all-out ideological war to "de-Nazify" the Germans, aggressively razing all symbols of Nazism while raising a new generation thoroughly educated of its evils. Yet, by the time the Berlin Blockade was over, the Allies found themselves

with a hard choice: to make friends with the Germans, including those who may have been Nazi sympathizers or Nazis themselves, or to alienate the Germans and risk ceding their hold on West Berlin to the Soviets. They took the first choice for many reasons. I.e., from conscripting to their cause prominent Nazis like Klaus Barbie (former head of a Gestapo office in France, known as "The Butcher of Lyon," who arrested and tortured more than 10,000 men, women and children, including dozens of orphaned Jewish children before deporting them to death camps) and rocket scientist Werner von Braun (inventor of the V-2 rocket, whom the U.S. conscripted to develop missile systems, as well as the Saturn-V rocket used to launch the Apollo spacecraft that landed on the moon, yet whose slave labor camps during the Holocaust were notorious for their brutality), to generally looking the other way, and even embracing Germans, regardless of their possible Nazi pasts.

If it wasn't taking the high moral ground, it was pragmatic. The new enemy was the Soviet Union, who, if they had their way, would absorb all Europe into one vast Communist Empire.

95 In August 1991, hard-line communists attempted a coup by kidnapping Gorbachev and insisting he hand the government over to them. Russian citizens took to the streets in protest. Soviet tanks appeared, threatening to put down the rebellion with force. The protesters met the tanks with flowers, arguing with their fellow compatriots manning the guns that the time for the end of the Soviet Union had arrived. Defying orders at times, the Soviet troops let the demonstrators be and did nothing. Realizing their coup had failed, the insurgents released Gorbachev.

However, he was now powerless. The people were demanding the end of communism. Gorbachev resisted, arguing that his reforms were all that was necessary, not a complete revolution. An opposition leader, Boris Yeltsin, arose. Finally, on December 25, 1991, Gorbachev resigned and Yeltsin, who had banned the Communist Party a month earlier, took over. The next day, the Supreme Soviet, the legislative body that formally held all the power in the country, dissolved itself. The Soviet Union was officially dead.

96 Jews suffered horrifically during fighting between the communists and anti-communists (the Nationalists). In the Ukraine alone, over 150,000 Jews were massacred in pogroms—the Ukrainians considered every Jew a communist. Tens of thousands of widows and orphans were without homes or resources.

97 Communism, an idea first put into writing in the 1800s by Karl Marx, a German Jew who was a convert to Christianity, is a system of government that tries to spread wealth equally; no one is too rich or too poor. While that may sound nice, in reality, the way the rulers invariably accomplished this was to

keep everyone equally poor. They also had to have strict control over everyone's lives. This meant there would be no true equality. Those in government positions would be "more equal than others." They could arrest others for little or no reason, including practicing religion. Not all the negative repercussions of communism were obvious at the beginning. Communist ideals sounded good to many Jews and non-Jews. And even if people thought it wasn't perfect, they thought nothing could be worse than living under the Czars.

98 "When the communists seized power, all Jewish organizations, religious and non-religious, were banned. Conversely, anyone willing to follow the communist line was appointed to a respected position, granted privileges and publicly honored. The easy life of Communist Party members contrasted sharply with the widespread struggle to survive. Some of the Zionists and *Maskilim* ("Enlightened" Jews) decided to take the path of least resistance and join the Communist Party. These new converts to communism were taken in by Lenin's promises of equality to the Jews. They felt they could maintain their Jewish identity and still be accepted if they went along with the communist ideology. It was this group that formed the nucleus of the infamous Yevsektzia, whose aim was to indoctrinate the Jews in Party ideals. The communists would probably have been as powerless as the Czars to destroy the Jewish faith, were it not for the Yevsektzia. Before long, there were branches of the Yevsektzia in every town and village. The Yevsektzia acted with lightning speed. *Chadorim* (Jewish elementary schools) and *yeshivos* were immediately closed. Anti-religious papers and journals were published, with such names as *Emes* (truth) and *Stern* (star). One was even called *Apikores* (heretic). Its cover featured a picture of a spear piercing a small circle containing a bearded religious Jew and a Star of David." (From *Deep In The Russian Night*, by Aaron Chazan)

99 The root of the Communist ideal's bankruptcy was extant from its inception, by a mistaken assumption of its founder. Essayist Sarah Yocheved Rigler—a self-acclaimed former leftist radical turned *baalas teshuva*—summarized this nicely in her article, "My Guru, Dr. Jacobs" (Aish.com, Jan. 30, 2005): "Karl Marx taught that economics is the driving force in human affairs ... Marx missed the mark because his doctrine, aptly called Dialectical Materialism, takes into account only the materialistic, most superficial, level of reality. Judaism, on the other hand, addresses itself to the spiritual sub-stratum of reality, where compassion and selflessness are a more valued currency than dollars and cents. If Marx were right, all rich people would be happy. Instead, Judaism is right: all loved people [i.e., all who love and are beloved] are happy."

100 In truth, a great "Spiritual Revolution" among Jews began to take root in the dark days under Josef Stalin. The worst crime in the Soviet Union's eyes was to teach Torah. Jews were not allowed any type of formal Jewish education under

Communism. If anyone wanted to learn anything about Judaism, they had to go to secret classes at the risk of imprisonment or even death.

Rabbi Avrohom Miller had been a close *talmid* (student) of the Chofetz Chaim. The KGB made an exception and allowed him to teach Torah classes in Moscow—but only as long as he did so in Yiddish. They knew the younger generation did not understand Yiddish, and might even be turned off by old Jews to whom they could not relate. In their mind, the Torah would be lost completely after the older generation died. However, Rabbi Miller fooled them. He would switch to Russian when he knew the KGB was not there.

Rabbi Miller had a student named Eliyahu Essas, who went on to teach Torah secretively to thousands of Jews in small groups. If someone wanted to learn in Eliyahu Essas' class, there was one condition. His students had to teach other Jews what they learned in his classes. Although the Israeli and Jewish media knew of Eliyahu Essas' activities, they did not publish his name or any article about his Torah classes, in order to protect him from arrest.

All this learning in secret was quietly producing a spiritual revolution in the Soviet Union. More and more people were tasting the sweetness of Torah, and finding pride in their Jewish identity. They began to realize that there was more to life than the values Soviet society force-fed them; that an idea could be stronger than an all-powerful government dedicated to oppression; that the State could take their freedom but not their *neshamos* (souls). Torah learning played the pivotal role in this newfound spiritual strength.

At this time, there arose a group of people called refuseniks. These were people who applied to the government for exit visas, which were documents giving them permission to leave the country. These were usually "refused." It took great courage and conviction to apply for an exit visa. Those who did risked losing their jobs while they were waiting to get visas, if they ever got them. Sometimes they were put in prison for daring to ask to leave the Soviet Union. A Jew thrown into prison for this reason became known as "a prisoner of Zion."

Eliyahu Essas was a famous refusenik. Anatoly Sharansky was another famous refusenik. He wanted to get out of the Soviet Union in 1970. Rather than wait for an exit visa, he decided to hijack a plane and land it in the West. His plot failed and he was caught. When he was sentenced, he stood before the court and said *Shema Yisrael*. Sharansky was eventually freed in 1981 and settled in *Eretz Yisrael*, where he served in the government.

The United States was very helpful toward Jews who wanted to leave the Soviet Union in the '60s and '70s. They put pressure on the Soviet Government to let the Jews leave. American Jews did other things to help the plight of Soviet Jews. Over a million Jews eventually left the Soviet Union, thanks to these efforts and *yad Hashem*.

After the Soviet Union fell, Jews still living there wanted to leave because of rising anti-Semitism among the Russian population. Most were too poor to leave, though. However, help came in the form of "operation open curtain," a campaign by American Jews to raise money to help Soviet Jews settle in America.

Many Jews from the former Soviet Union came to settle in Brooklyn, New York. Today there are hundreds of thousands of such Jews.

101 Some understand the Zohar as referring to the "sixth" century of the sixth millennium, which would correspond to the years 1740-1840.

102 Rabbi Mordechai Kaminetzky, *shlit"a*, related to me that his grandfather, HaRav Yaakov Kaminetzky, *zt"l*, had no problem with the idea of flying a space ship to the moon; it was a boost to Torah, not a challenge.

103 *Tosafos* (*Avodah Zarah* 41a) cite the *Talmud Yerushalmi* stating that Alexander ascended high above the earth and realized the Earth was round like a sphere.

104 Nevertheless, Orville wrote of his childhood: "We were lucky enough to grow up in an environment where there was always much encouragement to children to pursue intellectual interests; to investigate whatever aroused curiosity." Orville was apparently the less studious of the two, but he was "a champion bicyclist," which was how he and Wilbur entered the bicycle business.

105 This is reminiscent of the Talmudic teaching: "Open for me an opening the size of the eye of a needle and I will open for you an opening the size of the Temple hall" (*Shir Hashirim Rabbah* 5). The most important step in any journey is the first step, no matter how small it is.

106 "First Flight: How Wright Brothers Changed World," by Willie Drye for *National Geographic News*, December 17, 2003.

107 Nevertheless, even then some in the scientific world could not accept the fact that two "hobbyists" had accomplished what "scientists" could not. Most notably, the Smithsonian Institute insisted that the "Aerodrome"—made by then director Samuel P. Langley—was the "first man-carrying airplane capable of flight." Langley claimed to be the "father of flight," but his pre-Wright "Aerodrome" proved unable to sustain flight, and crashed into the Potomac River immediately upon launch from the top of a riverboat. It wasn't until 1942 (!) that the Smithsonian apologized and published a statement that unequivocally credited the Wright machine as the first airplane capable of flight. The Wrights, indeed, had applied for a patent on their machine—

whose then revolutionary principles of flight are still the mainstay of modern aerodynamics—as early as March 1903, nearly ten months before their first flight, but weren't granted a patent until May 22, 1906. Wilbur spent the last few years of his life fighting over the validity of the patent, and died without knowing whether the world fully acknowledged him and his brother as the inventors of the first true airplane. Only time and history could vindicate the Wrights.

108 The Wrights actually attempted to fly their machine three days earlier, on Monday, December 14, 1903 (the first day of *Chanukah*), but after the Flyer lifted off, it immediately sank down and was slightly damaged. By Thursday, it was repaired and ready to make history.

109 *A Night To Remember*, by Walter Lord, p. 42. Thirty-one years after writing *A Night To Remember*, Walter Lord authored *The Night Lives On*, which addressed three decades of theories and questions that never died about the *Titanic*. Among the questions was the assertion that the *Titanic* was never advertised as "unsinkable," and all claims to the effect were just "myth." Lord spends a couple of pages demonstrating that although the ship's builders, the White Star Line, never claimed the ship was unsinkable, it was nevertheless the "considered opinion of the experts of the time." (*The Night Lives On*, pp. 27-29).

110 Research subsequently discovered that the iceberg punctured several small holes in the ship, which all told amounted to little more than 12 square feet of damage—12 square feet that fatally spanned six otherwise watertight compartments.

111 After the sinking of the *Titanic*, a law was established that all ships had to have enough lifeboats for all passengers. The *Titanic* actually carried more lifeboats than required by law at that time.

112 All told, there were 37 seconds between spotting the iceberg and the collision. Spotting it perhaps 10 seconds earlier or later could have averted the disaster.

113 The sinking of the *Titanic* is sometimes called the end of the "Gilded Age," a name given to the period by Mark Twain and Charles Dudley Warner, who poked fun at the period for the rampant corruption at the end of the nineteenth century. During the "Gilded Age," the face of politics, business, technology and much more changed forever. It marked the advent of monopolies and the modern corporation, symbolized by the great railways that stretched across the vast plains of the U.S., breaking down the strict regional lines that had for so long defined culture and lifestyle. The economy became increasingly composed of managers and shareholders. Big business developed a mutual and corrupt alliance with politics, epitomized by such men as Boss Tweed,

who blatantly rigged and bought elections in New York, making a profit in the process.

Until the "Gilded Age," the U.S. had been an agrarian society: most of the population worked and lived on farms. By the end of the "Gilded Age," almost half the population lived in cities. Crowded inner-city slums developed. Upper class city-dwellers moved out into the suburbs, commuting by mass transit to work. The modern American city began to take shape.

The wealthy businessman symbolized both everything great and terrible in the modern world. On one hand, he represented progress. On the other hand, he represented excess, corruption and blatant disregard for the common person.

The nineteenth century began with enormous hope for and belief in the progress of human achievement. Social achievements like emancipation, equality and democracy, matched by the technological breakthroughs of the Industrial Revolution, were taken as sure signs that civilization was on the verge of a new age, an almost messianic-like era. By the turn of the twentieth century, however, racial and religious hatred, militarism, oppression of the disadvantaged, etc. had dampened if not effectively dashed the hopes of even the most "enlightened."

The *Titanic* was a temporary throwback to everything great the nineteenth century had envisioned: great technology, great wealth, great confidence in the achievements of the human race. As she sank to the bottom of the ocean, she took with her more than tons of metal and hundreds of lives. She took with her an era, an era that had grown overly reliant upon man-made progress— technological, social, political, cultural, etc. Those who saw the symbolism in the demise of the "unsinkable" ship sensed that civilization was on a collision course, not with redemption, but the iceberg of great misery—a misery caused by the very elements of "progress" people of the nineteenth century had pinned their hopes upon.

114 Commentators often identify water, one of the classic four elements, with *taaveh*, desire. Many teachings censure the Egyptians for their baseness, their sexual immorality and excessive pursuit of wealth. The material extravagances of those on board the *Titanic* have already been noted. It can be said, then, that both cultures ultimately were drowned by, through and in their own excessive material desires.

115 The brothers' great-grandfather, Jacob Lazare, was a member of the Assembly of Jewish Notables convened by Napoleon in Paris in 1806, which led to the establishment of the French Sanhedrin, created by Napoleon to advise him when he was considering the liberation of all Jews in his dominions. Their father,

Lazarus Straus, emigrated from Otterberg, Bavaria (now part of Germany) in 1852 to Talbotton, Georgia, where he later was joined by his wife and three sons, Isidore, Nathan and Oscar. He started out as a pushcart peddler, and later opened a dry goods store, although he was not allowed to own it because Jews couldn't own businesses there. He was an observant Jew in a place where there were no other Jews. The Straus family supported the Confederacy during the Civil War. Isidore worked as a Confederate bond salesman, and went to Europe to purchase supplies for the Confederate states, including ships for blockade running, but after the war ended, he settled in New York, where he became a partner in Macy's. He was a close, personal friend of President Grover Cleveland, and worked on Cleveland's re-election campaign of 1892, but turned down the position of Postmaster General, stating that he was "seeking neither glory nor office." He was elected to the House of Representatives in Congress from the 15th district of New York in 1892.

116 Later investigation would reveal that the explosion of the $1.2 billion spacecraft was due to a failure of two rubber "O-rings," essentially a $900 synthetic rubber band that seals the solid rocket fuel booster.

117 It would take seven months, 31 ships, 52 aircraft and 6,000 workers before the search for shuttle debris would be complete. Among the debris, Christa McAuliffe's lesson plans for space were found floating in the Atlantic Ocean. Forty days after the disaster, the crew compartment was found. When the bodies were brought up, it became clear that some of the astronauts had been alive during the three-to-four-minute fall to the sea.

118 Of course, it was and is dangerous to assume one understands the ways of *Hashem*. Even Moshe, according to one opinion at least, was not successful penetrating the veil that masks *Hashem*'s ways (*Berachos* 7a). Nevertheless, Rabbi Avigdor Miller writes, "by following the principles expounded by the Sages, we are able to discern the general plan" (*Rejoice O Youth*, p. 266). See the Introduction above. I cannot emphasize enough that here, as in all parts of this book where a connection to something in Torah is presented, the intention is to suggest a "point to ponder," rather than a definite correlation.

119 The *Challenger* disaster occurred on a Tuesday, the "third day" of the week. However, according to the Talmud, the third day, the day the Torah was given, was on *Shabbos*, the seventh day. (*Shabbos* 86b)

120 Officially designated the Strategic Defense Initiative (SDI), this was conceived as a space-based defense system to protect the U.S. from attack by nuclear missiles. Opponents dubbed it "Star Wars," after the blockbuster movie, implying that it was an impractical science fiction fantasy (but supporters adopted the usage as well). It's argued that it helped hasten the fall of the Soviet

Union by pressuring the communist superpower to keep pace with the U.S. in ways it could not afford.

121 See *Sefer Mitzvos Gadol (SMaG)*, Prohibition 1; see also the fifth of Maimonides' Thirteen Principles of Faith (found in his commentary to the Mishnah, *Sanhedrin* 10:1).

122 Including the "donkey" in yourself, your "inner" donkey.

123 As we know, each letter of the Hebrew alphabet has a numerical equivalent (*gematria*), and it is an age-old tradition to find allusions to deeper thoughts in the numerical value of a given word. Arguably, the most well-known *gematria* is the one for *Hashem*'s four-letter name, the Tetragrammaton: 26. Bearing that in mind, it struck me from the beginning that one could perhaps find significance in the fact that the *Challenger* was the 25th shuttle mission. This seemed to me as if to say the mission was in some way a "challenge" to *Hashem*, an attempt to "touch" Him, to reach "26"—to in essence storm the heavens and replace Him with technological achievement. *Hashem*, of course, thwarted that before they could do so, before they could reach mission number 26. (That the shuttle program was eventually restarted does not detract from the fact that the disaster happened before they could reach number 26.)

124 Michael Foale, a British-born American astronaut serving on the International Space Station, where he was on a 200-day stay with a Russian cosmonaut, Alexander Kaleri, was asked by CNN about his impressions of the centennial anniversary of the Wright Brothers' first flight. He answered: "I think it's incredible when you think what's happened in a hundred years. It's astounding that maybe half a million people are in the air at any one time above our planet Earth—and that we, Alexander and myself, are two people living above the atmosphere, and moving around the Earth once every one and a half hours. When you think that that goes back to a twelve-second flight over 120 feet by Wilbur and Orville Wright in 1903, it is incredible."

125 See also *Zechariah* 12-14, *Yirmiyahu* 30, *Daniel* 11-12, *Yoel* 4 and *Tehillim* 83.

126 Rabbi Moshe Eisemann (commentary to Ezekiel, chapter 38, Mesorah Publications, Ltd.) goes into great depth about the identity of Gog and Magog, and the war represented by their names. *Bereishis* 10:2 identifies Magog as a descendant of Noah's son, Yefes. Yet, traditional sources name Amalek, Esav's grandson (*Bereishis* 36:12), as Israel's perennial archenemy who will try to annihilate them at the end of history. Why then is Yefes the one warring against the Jewish people in the "End of Days"? Rabbi Eisemann explains that the king and initiator of the campaign against Israel will be from Esav-Edom: "Gog." (According to the Septuagint, Gog is "Agag," a generic term used for

kings of Amalek.) The fighting force, however, will be drawn from the ranks of Yefes (as well as Ham and Ishmael's descendants). In Esther's time, the Amalekite Haman (descended from Esav) was the instigating force in the Persian (Yefes) court, and so it will be in the wars of Gog and Magog, when the Edomite king Gog will lead the Yefes nations to war.

Furthermore, Rabbi Eisemann explains, our Sages teach that Yefes' role in history is as the precursor of man's sense of the aesthetic. All appreciation of the arts, drama, poetry, music, athletics and philosophy has its roots in Yefes, the forerunner of Greece. These gifts are tools *Hashem* granted man. However, as Hirsch writes, "The seeker of beauty, the artist, is receptive to external stimuli." Yefes is pliable. He can place his gifts at Edom's feet as readily as he can subordinate them to Shem's striving for the Divine. Throughout history, we find Yefes fluctuating between the poles of true spirituality and the grossest sensuality. The same Yefes who allowed himself to be turned to holiness by his brother Shem was able, centuries later, to allow a Haman to control his empire, and attempt to wipe out Shem's descendants. When Gog will seek supporters in his final war against holiness and G-dliness, he will turn to the pliable Yefes.

This provides insight into another aspect of the wars of Gog and Magog. In the final struggle, Yefes—representative of all the worldly culture of which the human race is capable—will be joined with Edom. Man will have shown himself incapable of using these gifts in the service of holiness. (Rabbi Moshe Eisemann, commentary to *Yechezkel* 38:2, Mesorah Publications, Ltd.)

127 John Hersey, in his book on the subject, *Hiroshima*, noted a striking irony: "Miss Toshi Sasaki, clerk in a tinworks plant 1600 yards from the center of the catastrophe, was crushed when her room suddenly collapsed, and her left leg was pinned down by a falling bookcase. There, in the tin factory, in the first moment of the atomic age, a human being was crushed by books."

128 William L. Laurence, who described the blast from the bomb dropped on Nagasaki (three days after the Hiroshima bomb was dropped) in his Pulitzer Prize-winning article: "A Thousand Old Faithful Geysers Rolled Into One Blast," published in *The New York Times*, September 9, 1945.

129 *Loc. cit.* The same observer added: "It kept struggling in an elemental fury, like a creature in the act of breaking the bonds that held it down. In a few seconds it had freed itself from its gigantic stem and floated upward with tremendous speed, its momentum carrying it into the stratosphere to a height of about sixty thousand feet.

"But no sooner did this happen when another mushroom, smaller in size than the first one, began emerging out of the pillar. It was as though the decapitated monster was growing a new head.

"As the first mushroom floated off into the blue it changed its shape into a flower-like form, its giant petals curving downward, creamy white outside, rose-colored inside. It still retained that shape when we last gazed at it from a distance of about two hundred miles. The boiling pillar of many colors could also be seen at that distance, a giant mountain of jumbled rainbows, in travail. Much living substance had gone into those rainbows. The quivering top of the pillar was protruding to a great height through the white clouds, giving the appearance of a monstrous prehistoric creature with a ruff around its neck, a fleecy ruff extending in all directions, as far as the eye could see."

130 I heard from Rabbi Avrohom Sutton—one of the first researchers for the Discovery Seminars, and author of its workbook—that the Vilna Gaon wrote that technology would reach a point where the world could be destroyed in eight minutes.

131 Even after the Japanese surrender, Japanese officers were planning kamikaze strikes at the battleship on which the surrender documents would be signed.

132 In Potsdam, when Truman gleefully revealed to Stalin that the U.S. had successfully tested a bomb of "exceptional power," the Soviet leader didn't flinch. He and others (including Churchill) watching Stalin's face assumed the Soviet leader failed to fathom the significance of what he had heard. In actual fact, Stalin knew all about the bomb and, upon returning to his quarters, immediately told his close advisors to speed up their own development of the bomb.

133 According to the World Health Organization, a nuclear exchange at the time would have meant roughly 300 million people killed, plus 300 million seriously injured! Some 50 million died in World War II.

134 Experts had predicted that they couldn't possibly make an atomic bomb until the mid-1950s. It's now known that the reason they were able to catch up so fast is because one of the developers of the atomic bomb passed its secrets to the Soviets.

135 In November 1952, the U.S. had become the first country to successfully explode a hydrogen bomb (H-bomb).

136 Sputnik pushed the U.S. to move full force into the Space Race. Not until the moon landings in 1969 could it be said that the Sputnik crisis had ended.

137 Tellingly, the strategy of deterrence underlying the proliferation of nuclear weapons was called M.A.D., standing for "Mutually Assured Destruction."

138 In 1961, he and U.S. president John F. Kennedy met for the first time in Vienna. For decades, Khrushchev, a man of humble peasant origins, had risen through the ranks of the brutal Soviet power hierarchy. Kennedy was a new president, a young man, a child of wealth. When they met for the first time, Kennedy, as host, stood up to shake Khrushchev's hand. Khrushchev regarded this as a sign of weakness, a sign that his counterpart in the U.S. was a person who could perhaps be bullied or persuaded regarding American foreign policy.

139 When Eisenhower yielded the presidency to Kennedy, the United States had around 18,000 nuclear weapons. Though the total Soviet arsenal did not match America's, they possessed enough nuclear bombs to lay waste to the Northern Hemisphere if they used them.

140 One of the campaign issues in the 1960 elections between Kennedy and Richard Nixon was the "missile gap." In actuality, there was no gap. The Americans were well ahead of the Soviets. (In the Americans defense, however, they did not find this out for certain until their new spy satellites gathered information after the 1960 election.)

141 Kennedy aide and historian Arthur Schlesinger said: "This was not only the most dangerous moment of the Cold War. It was the most dangerous moment in human history."

142 Also on that day, a U.S. destroyer dropped depth charges on a Soviet submarine carrying a nuclear weapon. The U.S. Navy "did not have a clue that the submarine had a nuclear weapon on board." The depth charges "... exploded right next to the hull," the sub's signals intelligence officer Vadim Orlov said in an account reported by Reuters (Oct. 12, 2002). "It felt like you were sitting in a metal barrel, which somebody is constantly blasting with a sledgehammer." The Soviet submarine's crew thought the war may have started and considered using their nuclear weapon, but decide instead to surface, Orlov said.

143 If the U.S.S.R. declared it publicly, the U.S. would deny it, Kennedy told Dobrynin. In truth, the missiles in Turkey were obsolete, but the U.S. did not want to lose credibility. This solution was therefore acceptable to them.

144 Throughout the entire crisis—unknown to all but Kennedy, his secretary and possibly his brother Robert—the historic, behind-closed-door discussions that went into the decision-making were being taped by hidden microphones placed in the Oval Office. More than twenty-three hours of meetings and telephone calls were recorded, all of which have been painstakingly transcribed and documented in *The Kennedy Tapes: Inside The*

White House During The Cuban Missile Crisis, by Ernest May and Philip Zelikow (Harvard University Press, 1997).

145 Kennedy himself had said in his dramatic speech to the nation on October 22: "The 1930s taught us a clear lesson: aggressive conduct, if allowed to go unchecked and unchallenged, ultimately leads to war."

146 In Kennedy's thought process was the knowledge that his father, a highly influential American leader, was a leading and vocal supporter of Neville Chamberlain's policy of appeasement.

147 The U.S. kept as many as 180 B-52 bombers carrying nuclear bombs in the air *flying at all times*. Fully loaded with nuclear bombs, they would fly (often refueled in midair) to a preassigned line a certain distance from the Soviet Union and then, unless ordered to proceed, would turn around and fly back. At one point, SAC bombers deliberately flew past their turnaround points, and only turned around when the Soviet freighters carrying the missiles to Cuba stopped dead in the Atlantic.

148 *The Kennedy Tapes: Inside The White House During The Cuban Missile Crisis*, pp. 13-14.

149 Ibid., p. 14.

150 Ibid., p. 15.

151 The IDF claims two were killed, others report only one.

152 It should be noted that Rabbi Chaim Shmuelevitz, *zt"l*, in his *Sichos Mussar*, interprets the *Midrash* in *ascending* order.

GLOSSARY

Baal teshuva—a Jew who returns to mitzvah observance

Beis Hamikdash—the Holy Temple in Jerusalem

Bereishis—Genesis

Bitachon—trust

Chanukah—Hanukkah

Chazal—the Sages

Cheshvan—the second month of the Jewish year, counting from Rosh Hashanah

Devarim—Deuteronomy

Emunah—faith

Eretz Yisrael—the land of Israel

Hashem—G-d

Hashgachah—providence, supervision

Hoshana Rabba—the seventh day of Sukkos

Iyar—the eighth month of the Jewish year, counting from Rosh Hashanah

Kislev—the third month of the Jewish year, counting from Rosh Hashanah

Mashiach—the Messiah

Matan Torah—the giving of the Torah on Mount Sinai

Menorah—candelabra in the Holy Temple in Jerusalem; Jews light a similar candelabra on the holiday of Chanukah

Midrash—books of Biblical homiletics

Mishlei—Proverbs

Navi—prophet

Nisan—the seventh month of the Jewish year, counting from Rosh Hashanah

Parashah—the weekly Torah portion read in synagogues

Pesach—Passover

Rashi—Rabbi Shlomo Yitzchaki, classic commentator on the Torah, Prophets, Writings and the Talmud

Sephardic—pertaining to Jews who trace their ancestry to Spain, North Africa and other Mediterranean countries

Shabbos—the Sabbath

Shavuos—the Festival of Weeks, which commemorates the giving of the Torah on Mount Sinai

Shemos—Exodus

Shofar—ram's horn, traditionally blown on the holiday of Rosh Hashanah

Sukkos—the Festival of Tabernacles, which commemorates how Hashem sheltered the Jewish people in the desert for forty years

Tammuz—the tenth month of the Jewish year, counting from Rosh Hashanah

Tanach—acronym for Torah (the Five Books of Moses), Neviim (the Prophets) and Kesuvim (the Holy Writings)

Tehillim—Psalms

Vayikra—Leviticus

Yad Hashem—the hand of Hashem, referring to Divine Providence

Yeshiva—Torah school

Yom Kippur—the Day of Atonement, which falls on the tenth of the month of Tishrei

Zt"l—acronym for *"zecher tzaddik livracha,"* may the memory of the righteous be for a blessing